FOREWORD

The collection of "Everything Will Be Okay" travel phrasebooks published by T&P Books is designed for people traveling abroad for tourism and business. The phrasebooks contain what matters most - the essentials for basic communication. This is an indispensable set of phrases to "survive" while abroad.

This phrasebook will help you in most cases where you need to ask something, get directions, find out how much something costs, etc. It can also resolve difficult communication situations where gestures just won't help.

This book contains a lot of phrases that have been grouped according to the most relevant topics. A separate section of the book also provides a small dictionary with more than 1,500 important and useful words.

Take "Everything Will Be Okay" phrasebook with you on the road and you'll have an irreplaceable traveling companion who will help you find your way out of any situation and teach you to not fear speaking with foreigners.

TABLE OF CONTENTS

Pronunciation 5
List of abbreviations 6
English-Kyrgyz phrasebook 7
Concise Dictionary 73

T&P Books Publishing

T&P Books Publishing

PHRASEBOOK

— KYRGYZ —

THE MOST IMPORTANT PHRASES

This phrasebook contains
the most important
phrases and questions
for basic communication
Everything you need
to survive overseas

T&P BOOKS

By Andrey Taranov

Phrasebook + 1500-word dictionary

English-Kyrgyz phrasebook & concise dictionary

By Andrey Taranov

The collection of "Everything Will Be Okay" travel phrasebooks published by T&P Books is designed for people traveling abroad for tourism and business. The phrasebooks contain what matters most - the essentials for basic communication. This is an indispensable set of phrases to "survive" while abroad.

Another section of the book also provides a small dictionary with more than 1,500 useful words arranged alphabetically. The dictionary includes a lot of gastronomic terms and will be helpful when ordering food at a restaurant or buying groceries at the store.

T&P Books Publishing
www.tpbooks.com

ISBN: 978-1-78767-149-2

This book is also available in E-book formats.
Please visit www.tpbooks.com or the major online bookstores.

PRONUNCIATION

T&P phonetic alphabet	Kyrgyz example	English example
[a]	манжа [mandʒa]	shorter than in ask
[e]	келечек [keletʃek]	elm, medal
[i]	жигит [dʒigit]	shorter than in feet
[ı]	кубаныч [kubanıtʃ]	big, America
[o]	мактоо [maktoo]	pod, John
[u]	узундук [uzunduk]	book
[ʉ]	алюминий [alʉminij]	youth, usually
[y]	түнкү [tynky]	fuel, tuna
[b]	ашкабак [aʃkabak]	baby, book
[d]	адам [adam]	day, doctor
[dʒ]	жыгач [dʒıgatʃ]	joke, general
[f]	флейта [flejta]	face, food
[g]	тегерек [tegerek]	game, gold
[j]	бөйрөк [bøjrøk]	yes, New York
[k]	карапа [karapa]	clock, kiss
[l]	алтын [altın]	lace, people
[m]	бешмант [beʃmant]	magic, milk
[n]	найза [najza]	name, normal
[ŋ]	булуң [buluŋ]	ring
[p]	пайдубал [pajdubal]	pencil, private
[r]	рахмат [raxmat]	rice, radio
[s]	сагызган [sagızgan]	city, boss
[ʃ]	бурулуш [buruluʃ]	machine, shark
[t]	түтүн [tytyn]	tourist, trip
[x]	пахтадан [paxtadan]	hot, hobby
[ts]	шприц [ʃprits]	cats, tsetse fly
[tʃ]	биринчи [birintʃi]	church, French
[v]	квартал [kvartal]	very, river
[z]	казуу [kazuu]	zebra, please
[ʲ]	руль, актёр [rulʲ, aktʲor]	palatalization sign

LIST OF ABBREVIATIONS

English abbreviations

ab.	-	about
adj	-	adjective
adv	-	adverb
anim.	-	animate
as adj	-	attributive noun used as adjective
e.g.	-	for example
etc.	-	et cetera
fam.	-	familiar
fem.	-	feminine
form.	-	formal
inanim.	-	inanimate
masc.	-	masculine
math	-	mathematics
mil.	-	military
n	-	noun
pl	-	plural
pron.	-	pronoun
sb	-	somebody
sing.	-	singular
sth	-	something
v aux	-	auxiliary verb
vi	-	intransitive verb
vi, vt	-	intransitive, transitive verb
vt	-	transitive verb

KYRGYZ PHRASEBOOK

This section contains
important phrases that may
come in handy in various
real-life situations.
The phrasebook will help
you ask for directions, clarify
a price, buy tickets, and
order food at a restaurant

T&P Books Publishing

PHRASEBOOK
CONTENTS

The bare minimum 10

Questions 13

Needs 14

Asking for directions 16

Signs 18

Transportation. General phrases 20

Buying tickets 22

Bus 24

Train 26

On the train. Dialogue (No ticket) 28

Taxi 30

Hotel 32

Restaurant 35

Shopping 37

In town 39

Money 41

Time   43
Greetings. Introductions   45
Farewells   47
Foreign language   49
Apologies   50
Agreement   51
Refusal. Expressing doubt   52
Expressing gratitude   54
Congratulations. Best wishes   55
Socializing   56
Sharing impressions. Emotions   59
Problems. Accidents   61
Health problems   64
At the pharmacy   67
The bare minimum   69

T&P Books Publishing

The bare minimum

Excuse me, ...

Кечиресиз, ...
ketʃiresiz, ...

Hello.

Саламатсызбы.
salamatsızbı.

Thank you.

Рахмат.
raχmat.

Good bye.

Көрүшкөнчө.
køryʃkønʧø.

Yes.

Ооба.
ooba.

No.

Жок.
dʒok.

I don't know.

Мен билбейм.
men bilbejm.

Where? | Where to? | When?

Каякта? | Каякка? | Качан?
kajakta? | kajakka? | katʃan?

I need ...

Мага ... керек эле.
maga ... kerek ele.

I want ...

Мен ... гым келет.
men ... gım kelet.

Do you have ...?

Силерде ... барбы?
silerde ... barbı?

Is there a ... here?

Бул жерде ... барбы?
bul dʒerde ... barbı?

May I ...?

Мага ... болобу?
maga ... bolobu?

..., please (polite request)

Сураныч
suranıʧ

I'm looking for ...

Мен ... издеп жаттым эле.
men ... izdep dʒattım ele.

the restroom

даараткана
daaratkana

an ATM

банкомат
bankomat

a pharmacy (drugstore)

дарыкана
darıkana

a hospital

оорукана
oorukana

the police station

милиция бөлүмү
militsija bølymy

the subway

метро
metro

a taxi	**такси** taksi
the train station	**вокзал** vokzal

My name is …	**Менин атым …** menin atım …
What's your name?	**Сиздин атыңыз ким?** sizdin atıŋız kim?
Could you please help me?	**Мага жардам берип коюңузчу.** maga dʒardam berip kodʒʉŋuztʃu.
I've got a problem.	**Менде көйгөй чыкты.** mende køygøj tʃıktı.
I don't feel well.	**Мен өзүмдү жаман сезип жатам.** men øzymdy dʒaman sezip dʒatam.
Call an ambulance!	**Тез жардамды чакырып коюңузчу!** tez dʒardamdı tʃakırıp kodʒʉŋuztʃu!
May I make a call?	**Телефон чалып алсам болобу?** telefon tʃalıp alsam bolobu?

I'm sorry.	**Кечирип коюңуз** ketʃirip kojʉŋuz
You're welcome.	**Эчтеке эмес** etʃteke emes

I, me	**мен** men
you (inform.)	**сен** sen
he	**ал** al
she	**ал** al
they (masc.)	**алар** alar
they (fem.)	**алар** alar
we	**биз** biz
you (pl)	**сиз** siz
you (sg, form.)	**Сиз** siz

ENTRANCE	**КИРҮҮ** kiryy
EXIT	**ЧЫГУУ** tʃıguu
OUT OF ORDER	**ИШТЕБЕЙТ** iʃtebejt
CLOSED	**ЖАБЫК** dʒabık

OPEN

АЧЫК
atʧık

FOR WOMEN

АЙЫМДАР ҮЧҮН
ajımdar yʧyn

FOR MEN

ЭРКЕКТЕР ҮЧҮН
erkekter yʧyn

Questions

Where? | **Каякта?**
kajakta?

Where to? | **Кайда?**
kajda?

Where from? | **Каяктан?**
kajaktan?

Why? | **Эмне үчүн?**
emne ytʃyn?

For what reason? | **Эмнеге?**
emnege?

When? | **Качан?**
katʃan?

How long? | **Канчага?**
kantʃaga?

At what time? | **Саат канчада?**
saat kantʃada?

How much? | **Канча турат?**
kantʃa turat?

Do you have ...? | **Силерде ... барбы?**
silerde ... barbı?

Where is ...? | **... каякта жайгашкан?**
... kajakta dʒajgaʃkan?

What time is it? | **Саат канча болду?**
saat kantʃa boldu?

May I make a call? | **Телефон чалып алсам болобу?**
telefon tʃalıp alsam bolobu?

Who's there? | **Ким бул?**
kim bul?

Can I smoke here? | **Бул жерде тамеки чексем болобу?**
bul dʒerde tameki tʃeksem bolobu?

May I ...? | **Мага ... болобу?**
maga ... bolobu?

Needs

I'd like …	**Мен … дедим эле.** men … dedim ele.
I don't want …	**Мен … келген жок.** men … kelgen dʒok.
I'm thirsty.	**Мен ичким келет.** men itʃkim kelet.
I want to sleep.	**Мен уйкум келет.** men ujkum kelet.

I want …	**Мен …** men …
to wash up	**жуунуп алайын дедим эле** dʒuunup alajın dedim ele
to brush my teeth	**тишимди тазалап алайын дедим эле** tiʃimdi tazalap alajın dedim ele
to rest a while	**бир аз эс алгым келип жатат** bir az es algım kelip dʒatat
to change my clothes	**кийимимди которуп алайын дедим эле** kijimimdi kotorup alajın dedim ele
to go back to the hotel	**мейманканага кайра кетким келет** mejmankanaga kajra ketkim kelet
to buy …	**… сатып алгым келет** … satıp algım kelet
to go to …	**… барып келгим келет** … barıp kelgim kelet
to visit …	**… көрүп келсемби дейм** … kørjp kelsembi dejm
to meet with …	**… менен жолугайын дейм** … menen dʒolugajın dejm
to make a call	**чалайын дейм** tʃalajın dejm

I'm tired.	**Мен чарчадым.** men tʃartʃadım.
We are tired.	**Биз чарчадык.** biz tʃartʃadık.
I'm cold.	**Мен үшүп кеттим.** men yʃyp kettim.
I'm hot.	**Мен ысып кеттим.** men ısıp kettim.
I'm OK.	**Баары жакшы.** baarı dʒakʃı.

I need to make a call.	**Мен чалышым керек.** men tʃalıʃım kerek.
I need to go to the restroom.	**Мен дааратканага барышым керек.** men daaratkanaga barıʃim kerek.
I have to go.	**Мен кетишим керек.** men ketiʃim kerek.
I have to go now.	**Мен азыр кетишим керек.** men azır ketiʃim kerek.

Asking for directions

Excuse me, ...
Кечиресиз, ...
ketʃiresiz, ...

Where is ...?
... каякта жайгашкан?
... kajakta dʒajgaʃkan?

Which way is ...?
... кайсы жакта жайгашканын билбейсизби?
... kajsı dʒakta dʒajgaʃkanın bilbejsizbi?

Could you help me, please?
Мага жардам берип коюнузчу.
maga dʒardam berip kodʒuŋuzʧu.

I'm looking for ...
Мен ... издеп жаттым эле.
men ... izdep dʒattım ele.

I'm looking for the exit.
Каяктан чыксам болот?
kajaktan ʧıksam bolot?

I'm going to ...
Мен ... кетип баратам.
men ... ketip baratam.

Am I going the right way to ...?
... жакка туура баратамбы?
... dʒakka tuura baratambı?

Is it far?
Бул жерден алыспы?
bul dʒerden alıspı?

Can I get there on foot?
Мен ал жакка жөө жете аламбы?
men al dʒakka dʒøø dʒete alambı?

Can you show me on the map?
Ал жакты картадан көрсөтүп бериңизчи.
al dʒaktı kartadan kørsøtyp beriŋizʧi.

Show me where we are right now.
Биз азыр кайсы жерде турабыз, көрсөтүп бериңизчи.
biz azır kajsı dʒerde turabız, kørsøtyp beriŋizʧi.

Here
Бул жерде
bul dʒerde

There
Тээтиги жерде
teetigi dʒerde

This way
Бул жак менен
bul dʒak menen

Turn right.
Азыр оңго.
azır oŋgo.

Turn left.
Азыр солго.
azır solgo.

first (second, third) turn

биринчи (экинчи, үчүнчү) бурулуш
birintʃi (ekintʃi, ytʃyntʃy) buruluʃ

to the right

оңго
oŋgo

to the left

солго
solgo

Go straight ahead.

Түз барыңыз.
tyz barıŋız.

Signs

WELCOME!	**КОШ КЕЛИҢИЗДЕР!** koʃ keliŋizder!
ENTRANCE	**КИРҮҮ** kiryy
EXIT	**ЧЫГУУ** ʧɪguu
PUSH	**ТҮРТҮҢҮЗ** tyrtyŋyz
PULL	**ТАРТЫҢЫЗ** tartɪŋɪz
OPEN	**АЧЫК** aʧɪk
CLOSED	**ЖАБЫК** dʒabɪk
FOR WOMEN	**АЙЫМДАР ҮЧҮН** ajɪmdar yʧyn
FOR MEN	**ЭРКЕКТЕР ҮЧҮН** erkekter yʧyn
GENTLEMEN, GENTS	**ЭРКЕКТЕР ДААРАТКАНАСЫ** erkekter daaratkanasɪ
WOMEN	**АЙЫМДАР ДААРАТКАНАСЫ** ajɪmdar daaratkanasɪ
DISCOUNTS	**АРЗАНДАТУУЛАР** arzandatuular
SALE	**САТЫП ТҮГӨТҮҮ** satɪp tygøtyy
FREE	**БЕКЕР** beker
NEW!	**СААМАЛЫК!** saamalɪk!
ATTENTION!	**КӨҢҮЛ БУРУҢУЗ!** køŋyl buruŋuz!
NO VACANCIES	**ОРУН ЖОК** orun dʒok
RESERVED	**КАМДЫК БУЙРУТМАЛАГАН** kamdɪk bujrutmalagan
ADMINISTRATION	**АДМИНИСТРАЦИЯ** administraʦija
STAFF ONLY	**ЖААМАТ ҮЧҮН ГАНА** dʒaamat yʧyn gana

BEWARE OF THE DOG!	**КАБАНААК ИТ** kabanaak it
NO SMOKING!	**ТАМЕКИ ЧЕГҮҮГӨ БОЛБОЙТ!** tameki ʧegyygø bolbojt!
DO NOT TOUCH!	**КОЛУҢАР МЕНЕН КАРМАБАГЫЛА!** koluŋar menen karmabagıla!
DANGEROUS	**КОРКУНУЧ БАР** korkunuʧ bar
DANGER	**КОРКУНУЧТУУ** korkunuʧtuu
HIGH VOLTAGE	**ЖОГОРКУ ЧЫҢАЛУУ** dʒogorku ʧıŋaluu
NO SWIMMING!	**СУУГА ТҮШҮҮГӨ БОЛБОЙТ** suuga tyʃyygø bolbojt

OUT OF ORDER	**ИШТЕБЕЙТ** iʃtebejt
FLAMMABLE	**ӨРТ ЧЫГУУ КОРКУНУЧУ** ørt ʧıguu korkunuʧu
FORBIDDEN	**БОЛБОЙТ** bolbojt
NO TRESPASSING!	**ӨТҮҮГӨ БОЛБОЙТ** øtyygø bolbojt
WET PAINT	**СЫРДАЛГАН** sırdalgan

CLOSED FOR RENOVATIONS	**ОҢДОО ИШТЕРИ ҮЧҮН ЖАБЫК** ondoo iʃteri yʧyn dʒabık
WORKS AHEAD	**ЖОЛ ОҢДОО ИШТЕРИ** dʒol oŋdoo iʃteri
DETOUR	**АЙЛАНЫП ӨТМӨ ЖОЛ** ajlanıp øtmø dʒol

Transportation. General phrases

plane	**самолёт** samolʲot
train	**поезд** poezd
bus	**автобус** avtobus
ferry	**паром** parom
taxi	**такси** taksi
car	**машина** maʃina

schedule	**ырааттама** ıraattama
Where can I see the schedule?	**Ырааттаманы кайсыл жерден көрсөм болот?** iraattamanı kajsıl dʒerden kørsøm bolot?
workdays (weekdays)	**иш күндөрү** iʃ kyndøry
weekends	**эс алуу күндөрү** es aluu kyndøry
holidays	**майрам күндөрү** majram kyndøry

DEPARTURE	**ЖӨНӨӨ** dʒønøø
ARRIVAL	**КЕЛҮҮ** kelyy
DELAYED	**КАРМАЛУУ** karmaluu
CANCELLED	**ЖОККО ЧЫГАРЫЛГАН** dʒokko tʃıgarılgan

next (train, etc.)	**кийинки** kijinki
first	**биринчи** birintʃi
last	**акыркы** akırkı

When is the next ...?

Кийинки ... качан келет?
kijinki ... katʃan kelet?

When is the first ...?

Биринчи ... качан кетет?
birintʃi ... katʃan ketet?

When is the last ...?

Акыркы ... качан кетет?
akırkı ... katʃan ketet?

transfer (change of trains, etc.)

которулуп түшүү
kotorulup tyʃyy

to make a transfer

которулуп түшүү
kotorulup tyʃyy

Do I need to make a transfer?

Которулуп түшүшүм керекпи?
kotorulup tyʃyʃym kerekpi?

Buying tickets

Where can I buy tickets?	**Билетти каяктан сатып алсам болот.** biletti kajaktan satıp alsam bolot.
ticket	**билет** bilet
to buy a ticket	**билетти сатып алуу** biletti satıp aluu
ticket price	**билеттин баасы** bilettin baası
Where to?	**Кайда?** kajda?
To what station?	**Кайсы станцияга чейин?** kajsı stantsijaga ʧejin?
I need ...	**Мага ... керек.** maga ... kerek.
one ticket	**бир билет** bir bilet
two tickets	**эки билет** eki bilet
three tickets	**үч билет** yʧ bilet
one-way	**бир тарапка** bir tarapka
round-trip	**барып келүү** barıp kelyy
first class	**биринчи класс** birinʧi klass
second class	**экинчи класс** ekinʧi klass
today	**бүгүн** bygyn
tomorrow	**эртең** erteŋ
the day after tomorrow	**бүрсүгүнү** byrsygyny
in the morning	**эртең менен** erteŋ menen
in the afternoon	**күндүз** kyndyz
in the evening	**кечинде** keʧinde

aisle seat

кире бериш жактагы орун
kire beriʃ ʤaktagı orun

window seat

терезе жанындагы орун
tereze ʤanındagı orun

How much?

Канча турат?
kanʧa turat?

Can I pay by credit card?

Карточка менен төлөсөм болобу?
kartoʧka menen tøløsøm bolobu?

Bus

bus	**автобус** avtobus
intercity bus	**шаар аралык автобус** ʃaar aralık avtobus
bus stop	**автобус аялдамасы** avtobus ajaldaması
Where's the nearest bus stop?	**Жакын арада автобустун аялдамасы барбы?** dʒakın arada avtobustun ajaldaması barbı?
number (bus ~, etc.)	**номер** nomer
Which bus do I take to get to ...?	**Кайсы автобус ... чейин барат?** kajsı avtobus ... tʃejin barat?
Does this bus go to ...?	**Бул автобус ... чейин барабы?** bul avtobus ... tʃejin barabı?
How frequent are the buses?	**Автобустар канчалык тез жүрүп турат?** avtobustar kantʃalık tez dʒyryp turat?
every 15 minutes	**он беш мүнөт сайын** on beʃ mynøt sajın
every half hour	**ар жарым саат сайын** ar dʒarım saat sajın
every hour	**ар бир саатта** ar bir saatta
several times a day	**бир күндө бир нече жолу** bir kyndø bir netʃe dʒolu
... times a day	**бир күндө ... жолу** bir kyndø ... dʒolu
schedule	**ырааттама** ıraattama
Where can I see the schedule?	**Ырааттаманы кайсыл жерден көрсөм болот?** iraattamanı kajsıl dʒerden kørsøm bolot?
When is the next bus?	**Кийинки автобус качан келет?** kijinki avtobus katʃan kelet?
When is the first bus?	**Биринчи автобус качан кетет?** birintʃi avtobus katʃan ketet?
When is the last bus?	**Акыркы автобус качан кетет?** akırkı avtobus katʃan ketet?

stop

аялдама
ajaldama

next stop

кийинки аялдама
kijinki ajaldama

last stop (terminus)

акыркы аялдама
akırkı ajaldama

Stop here, please.

Ушул жерден токтотуп койсоңуз.
uʃul dʒerden toktotup kojsoŋuz.

Excuse me, this is my stop.

Бул аялдамадан токтотуп коёсузбу?
bul ajaldamadan toktotup kojosuzbu?

Train

train	**поезд** poezd
suburban train	**шаардан тышкары барчу поезд** ʃaardan tıʃkarı barʧu poezd
long-distance train	**алыс аралыкка жүрүүчү поезд** alıs aralıkka dʒyryyʧy poezd
train station	**вокзал** vokzal
Excuse me, where is the exit to the platform?	**Кечиресиз, поезддер жакка кантип барсам болот?** ketʃiresiz, poezdder dʒakka kantip barsam bolot?
Does this train go to …?	**Бул поезд … чейин барабы?** bul poezd … ʧejin barabı?
next train	**кийинки поезд** kijinki poezd
When is the next train?	**Кийинки поезд качан келет?** kijinki poezd katʃan kelet?
Where can I see the schedule?	**Ыраатаманы кайсыл жерден көрсөм болот?** iraattamanı kajsıl dʒerden kørsøm bolot?
From which platform?	**Кайсы платформадан?** kajsı platformadan?
When does the train arrive in …?	**Поезд … качан келет?** poezd … katʃan kelet?
Please help me.	**Мага жардам берип коюнузчу.** maga dʒardam berip kodʒuŋuzʧu.
I'm looking for my seat.	**Мен өз ордумду издеп жаттым эле.** men øz ordumdu izdep dʒattım ele.
We're looking for our seats.	**Биз өз ордубузду издеп жатабыз.** biz øz ordubuzdu izdep dʒatabız.
My seat is taken.	**Менин ордум бош эмес.** menin ordum boʃ emes.
Our seats are taken.	**Биздин орундарыбыз бош эмес.** bizdin orundarıbız boʃ emes.
I'm sorry but this is my seat.	**Кечиресиз, бирок бул менин орунум.** ketʃiresiz, birok bul menin orunum.

Is this seat taken?

Бул орун бошпу?
bul orun boʃpu?

May I sit here?

Мен бул жерге отурсам болобу?
men bul ʤerge otursam bolobu?

On the train. Dialogue (No ticket)

Ticket, please.

Билетиңизди көрсөтүп коюңузчу.
biletiŋizdi körsötyp kojuŋuztʃu.

I don't have a ticket.

Менин билетим жок.
menin biletim dʒok.

I lost my ticket.

Мен билетимди жоготуп алдым.
men biletimdi dʒogotup aldım.

I forgot my ticket at home.

Мен билетимди үйгө унутуп коюптурмун.
men biletimdi yjgø unutup koju̯pturmun.

You can buy a ticket from me.

Сиз билетти менден сатып алсаңыз болот.
siz biletti menden satıp alsaŋız bolot.

You will also have to pay a fine.

Сиз дагы айып төлөшүңүз керек.
siz dagı ajıp tøløʃyŋyz kerek.

Okay.

Макул.
makul.

Where are you going?

Сиз каякка баратасыз?
siz kajakka baratasız?

I'm going to …

… чейин барам.
… tʃejin baram.

How much? I don't understand.

Канча турат? Түшүнбөй жатам.
kantʃa turat? tyʃynbøj dʒatam.

Write it down, please.

Жазып бериңизчи.
dʒazıp beriŋiztʃi.

Okay. Can I pay with a credit card?

Макул. Мен карточка менен төлөсөм болобу?
makul. men kartotʃka menen tøløsøm bolobu?

Yes, you can.

Ооба, болот.
ooba, bolot.

Here's your receipt.

Мына сиздин эсеп дүмүрчөгү.
mına sizdin esep dymyrtʃøgy.

Sorry about the fine.

Айып төлөгөнүңүз үчүн кечирим сурайм.
ajıp tøløgønyŋyz ytʃyn ketʃirim surajm.

That's okay. It was my fault.

Эч нерсе эмес. Мен өзүм күнөөлүмүн.
etʃ nerse emes. men øzym kynøølymyn.

Enjoy your trip.

Жолуңуз шыдыр болсун.
dʒoluŋuz ʃıdır bolsun.

Taxi

taxi	**такси** taksi
taxi driver	**таксист** taksist
to catch a taxi	**такси кармоо** taksi karmoo
taxi stand	**Такси токтоочу жай** taksi toktootʃu dʒaj
Where can I get a taxi?	**Таксини каяктан кармасам болот?** taksini kajaktan karmasam bolot?

to call a taxi	**такси чакыруу** taksi tʃakıruu
I need a taxi.	**Мага такси керек болуп жатат.** maga taksi kerek bolup dʒatat.
Right now.	**Азыр, тез арада.** azır, tez arada.
What is your address (location)?	**Сиздин дарегиңиз?** sizdin dareginiz?
My address is ...	**Менин дарегим ...** menin daregim ...
Your destination?	**Сиз каякка барасыз?** siz kajakka barasız?

Excuse me, ...	**Кечиресиз, ...** ketʃiresiz, ...
Are you available?	**Сиз бошсузбу?** siz boʃsuzbu?
How much is it to get to ...?	**... чейин канча болот?** ... tʃejin kantʃa bolot?
Do you know where it is?	**Ал жак каякта экенин сиз билесизби?** al dʒak kajakta ekenin siz bilesizbi?

Airport, please.	**Аэропортко жеткирип койсоңуз.** aeroportko dʒetkirip kojsoŋuz.
Stop here, please.	**Бул жерден токтотуп койсоңуз.** bul dʒerden toktotup kojsoŋuz.
It's not here.	**Бул жерде эмес.** bul dʒerde emes.
This is the wrong address.	**Бул туура эмес дарек.** bul tuura emes darek.

Turn left.	**Азыр солго.** azır solgo.
Turn right.	**Азыр оңго.** azır oŋgo.

How much do I owe you?	**Сизге канча төлөйм?** sizge kantʃa tøløjm?
I'd like a receipt, please.	**Мага чек берип коюнузчу.** maga tʃek berip kojʉŋuztʃu.
Keep the change.	**Ашкан акчаны жөн эле коюңуз.** aʃkan aktʃanı dʒøn ele kodʒʉŋuz.

Would you please wait for me?	**Мени күтүп туруңузчу.** meni kytyp turuŋuztʃu.
five minutes	**беш мүнөт** beʃ mynøt
ten minutes	**он мүнөт** on mynøt
fifteen minutes	**он беш мүнөт** on beʃ mynøt
twenty minutes	**жыйырма мүнөт** dʒıjırma mynøt
half an hour	**жарым саат** dʒarım saat

Hotel

Hello.	**Саламатсызбы.** salamatsızbı.
My name is …	**Менин атым …** menin atım …
I have a reservation.	**Мен бөлмөгө камдык буйрутма жасадым эле.** men bølmøgø kamdık bujrutma dʒasadım ele.
I need …	**Мага … керек эле.** maga … kerek ele.
a single room	**бир орундуу бөлмө** bir orunduu bølmø
a double room	**эки орундуу бөлмө** eki orunduu bølmø
How much is that?	**Ал канча турат?** al kantʃa turat?
That's a bit expensive.	**Бул бир аз кымбатыраак болуп калат.** bul bir az kımbatıraak bolup kalat.
Do you have anything else?	**Силерде дагы башка бөлмөлөр барбы?** silerde dagı baʃka bølmølør barbı?
I'll take it.	**Мен ошону алам.** men oʃonu alam.
I'll pay in cash.	**Мен накталай төлөйм.** men naktalaj tøløjm.
I've got a problem.	**Менде көйгөй чыкты.** mende køjgøj tʃıktı.
My … is broken.	**Менин … бузук экен.** menin … buzuk eken.
My … is out of order.	**Менин … иштебей жатат.** menin … iʃtebej dʒatat.
TV	**сыналгым** sınalgım
air conditioner	**аба салкындаткычым** aba salkındatkıtʃım
tap	**краным** kranım

shower	**душум** duʃum
sink	**раковинам** rakovinam
safe	**сейфим** sejfim
door lock	**кулпум** kulpum
electrical outlet	**розеткам** rozetkam
hairdryer	**чач кургаткычым** ʧaʧ kurgatkıʧim

I don't have …	**Менин … жок.** menin … dʒok.
water	**суу** suu
light	**жарык** dʒarık
electricity	**электр кубаты** elektr kubatı

Can you give me …?	**Мага … берип коесузбу?** maga … berip koesuzbu?
a towel	**сүлгү** sylgy
a blanket	**жууркан** dʒuurkan
slippers	**тапичке** tapiʧke
a robe	**халат** χalat
shampoo	**шампунь** ʃampunⁱ
soap	**самын** samın

I'd like to change rooms.	**Мен бөлмөмдү алмаштырайын дедим эле.** men bølmømdy almaʃtırajın dedim ele.
I can't find my key.	**Мен ачкычымды таппай жатам.** men aʧkıʧimdı tappaj dʒatam.
Could you open my room, please?	**Менин бөлмөмдү ачып берип коюңузчу.** menin bølmømdy aʧıp berip kojюŋuzʧu.
Who's there?	**Ким бул?** kim bul?
Come in!	**Кире бериңиз!** kire beriŋiz!

Just a minute! **Бир мүнөт!**
bir mynøt!

Not right now, please. **Кечиресиз, азыр эмес.**
ketʃiresiz, azır emes.

Come to my room, please. **Мага кирип койгулачы.**
maga kirip kojgulatʃı.

I'd like to order food service. **Мен тамакты бөлмөгө заказ
кылайын дегем.**
men tamaktı bølmøgø zakaz
kılajın degem.

My room number is … **Менин бөлмөмдүн номери …**
menin bølmømdyn nomeri …

I'm leaving … **Мен … кеткени жатам.**
men … ketkeni dʒatam.

We're leaving … **Биз … кеткени жатабыз.**
biz … ketkeni dʒatabız.

right now **азыр**
azır

this afternoon **бүгүн түштөн кийин**
bygyn tyʃtøn kijin

tonight **бүгүн кечинде**
bygyn ketʃinde

tomorrow **эртең**
erteŋ

tomorrow morning **эртең эртең менен**
erteŋ erteŋ menen

tomorrow evening **эртең кечинде**
erteŋ ketʃinde

the day after tomorrow **бүрсүгүнү**
byrsygyny

I'd like to pay. **Мен эсептешип коеюн дегем.**
men esepteʃip koejun degem.

Everything was wonderful. **Баары жакшы болду.**
baarı dʒakʃı boldu.

Where can I get a taxi? **Таксини каяктан кармасам болот?**
taksini kajaktan karmasam bolot?

Would you call a taxi for me, please? **Мага такси чакырып коюңузчу.**
maga taksi tʃakırıp kojuŋuztʃu.

Restaurant

Can I look at the menu, please?	**Силердин менюңерди көрсөм болобу?** silerdin menuŋerdi kørsøm bolobu?
Table for one.	**Бир кишилик стол керек.** bir kiʃilik stol kerek.
There are two (three, four) of us.	**Биз экөөбүз (үчөөбүз, төртөөбүз).** biz ekøøbyz (ytʃøøbyz, tørtøøbyz).
Smoking	**Тамеки чеккендер үчүн** tameki tʃekkender ytʃyn
No smoking	**Чекпегендер үчүн** tʃekpegender ytʃyn
Excuse me! (addressing a waiter)	**Кичипейилдикке!** kitʃipejildikke!
menu	**меню** menu
wine list	**шараптардын картасы** ʃaraptardın kartası
The menu, please.	**Менюну берип коюнузчу.** menunu berip kojuŋuztʃu.
Are you ready to order?	**Буйрутма бергенге даярсызбы?** bujrutma bergenge dajarsızbı?
What will you have?	**Буйрутмаңыз эмне болот?** bujrutmaŋız emne bolot?
I'll have ...	**Мен ... алам** men ... alam
I'm a vegetarian.	**Мен эт жебейм.** men et dʒebejm.
meat	**эт** et
fish	**балык** balık
vegetables	**жемиштер** dʒemiʃter
Do you have vegetarian dishes?	**Силерде эт кошулбаган тамактары барбы?** silerde et koʃulbagan tamaktarı barbı?
I don't eat pork.	**Мен чочконун этин жебейм.** men tʃotʃkonun etin dʒebejm.

Band-Aid	**Ал эт жебейт.** al et dʒebejt.
I am allergic to ...	**Менин ... аллергиям бар.** menin ... allergijam bar.

Would you please bring me ...	**Мага ... алып келип бериңизчи.** maga ... alıp kelip beriŋiztʃi.
salt | pepper | sugar	**туз | калемпир | кумшекер** tuz | kalempir | kumʃeker
coffee | tea | dessert	**кофе | чай | десерт** kofe | tʃaj | desert
water | sparkling | plain	**суу | газы менен | газы жок** suu | gazı menen | gazı dʒok
a spoon | fork | knife	**кашык | вилка | бычак** kaʃık | vilka | bıtʃak
a plate | napkin	**табак | салфетка** tabak | salfetka

Enjoy your meal!	**Тамагыңыз таттуу болсун!** tamagıŋız tattuu bolsun!
One more, please.	**Дагы алып келип бериңизчи.** dagı alıp kelip beriŋiztʃi.
It was very delicious.	**Аябай даамдуу болуптур.** ajabaj daamduu boluptur.

check | change | tip	**эсеп | ашкан акча | чайга** esep | aʃkan aktʃa | tʃajga
Check, please. (Could I have the check, please?)	**Эсептеп коюңузчу.** eseptep kojuŋuztʃu.
Can I pay by credit card?	**Карточка менен төлөсөм болобу?** kartotʃka menen tøløsøm bolobu?
I'm sorry, there's a mistake here.	**Кечиресиз, бул жакта ката кетип калыптыр.** ketʃiresiz, bul dʒakta kata ketip kalıptır.

Shopping

Can I help you?	**Сизге жардам берсем болобу?** sizge dʒardam bersem bolobu?
Do you have ...?	**Силерде ... барбы?** silerde ... barbɪ?
I'm looking for ...	**Мен ... издеп жаттым эле.** men ... izdep dʒattɪm ele.
I need ...	**Мага ... керек эле.** maga ... kerek ele.

I'm just looking.	**Мен жөн гана көрүп жатам.** men dʒøn gana køryp dʒatam.
We're just looking.	**Биз жөн гана көрүп жатабыз.** biz dʒøn gana køryp dʒatabɪz.
I'll come back later.	**Мен ананыраак келем.** men ananɪraak kelem.
We'll come back later.	**Биз ананыраак келебиз.** biz ananɪraak kelebiz.
discounts | sale	**арзандатуулар | сатып түгөтүү** arzandatuular | satɪp tygøtyy

Would you please show me ...	**Мага ... көрсөтүп коюңузчу.** maga ... kørsøtyp kojuŋuztʃu.
Would you please give me ...	**Мага ... берип коюңузчу.** maga ... berip kojuŋuztʃu.
Can I try it on?	**Мен кийип көрсөм болобу?** men kijip kørsøm bolobu?
Excuse me, where's the fitting room?	**Каяктан кийип көрсөм болот?** kajaktan kijip kørsøm bolot?
Which color would you like?	**Кайсыл өңүн каалап жатасыз?** kajsɪl øŋyn kaalap dʒatasɪz?
size | length	**өлчөм | бой** øltʃøm | boj
How does it fit?	**Чак келдиби?** tʃak keldibi?

How much is it?	**Бул канча турат?** bul kantʃa turat?
That's too expensive.	**Бул аябай кымбат.** bul ajabaj kɪmbat.
I'll take it.	**Мен муну сатып алам.** men munu satɪp alam.
Excuse me, where do I pay?	**Кечиресиз, касса кайсы жакта?** ketʃiresiz, kassa kajsɪ dʒakta?

Will you pay in cash or credit card?

Кандай төлөсүз? Накталайбы же карточка мененби?
kandaj tøløsyz? naktalajbı ʤe kartotʃka menenbi?

In cash | with credit card

накталай | карточка менен
naktalaj | kartotʃka menen

Do you want the receipt?

Сизге чек керекпи?
sizge tʃek kerekpi?

Yes, please.

Ооба, берип коюнузчу.
ooba, berip kojɯŋuztʃu.

No, it's OK.

Жок, кереги жок. Рахмат.
ʤok, keregi ʤok. raχmat.

Thank you. Have a nice day!

Рахмат. Жакшы калгыла.
raχmat. ʤakʃı kalgıla.

In town

Excuse me, …	**Кечиресиз, …** ketʃiresiz, …
I'm looking for …	**Мен … издеп жаттым эле.** men … izdep dʒattım ele.
the subway	**метрону** metronu
my hotel	**токтогон мейманканамды** toktogon mejmankanamdı
the movie theater	**кинотеатрды** kinoteatrdı
a taxi stand	**такси токтоочу жайды** taksi toktootʃu dʒajdı
an ATM	**банкоматты** bankomattı
a foreign exchange office	**акча алмаштыруу жайын** aktʃa almaʃtıruu dʒajın
an internet café	**интернет-кафени** internet-kafeni
… street	**… деген көчөнү** … degen køtʃøny
this place	**ушул орунду** uʃul orundu
Do you know where … is?	**Сиз … каякта экенин билесизби?** siz … kajakta ekenin bilesizbi?
Which street is this?	**Бул көчөнүн аталышы кандай?** bul køtʃønyn atalıʃı kandaj?
Show me where we are right now.	**Биз азыр кайсы жерде турабыз,** **көрсөтүп бериңизчи.** biz azır kajsı dʒerde turabız, kørsøtyp beriŋiztʃi.
Can I get there on foot?	**Мен ал жакка жөө жете аламбы?** men al dʒakka dʒøø dʒete alambı?
Do you have a map of the city?	**Сизде шаардын картасы барбы?** sizde ʃaardın kartası barbı?
How much is a ticket to get in?	**Кирүү билети канча турат?** kiryy bileti kantʃa turat?
Can I take pictures here?	**Бул жерде сүрөткө тартууга** **болобу?** bul dʒerde syrøtkø tartuuga bolobu?

Are you open?

Силер иштейсинерби?
siler iʃtejsinerbi?

When do you open?

Силер канчада ачыласынар?
siler kantʃada atʃɯlasɯnar?

When do you close?

Силер канчага чейин иштейсинер?
siler kantʃaga tʃejin iʃtejsiner?

Money

money	**акча** aktʃa
cash	**накталай акча** naktalaj aktʃa
paper money	**кагаз акча** kagaz aktʃa
loose change	**майда акча** majda aktʃa
check | change | tip	**эсеп | ашкан акча | чайга** esep | aʃkan aktʃa | tʃajga
credit card	**кредит карточкасы** kredit kartotʃkası
wallet	**капчык** kaptʃık
to buy	**сатып алуу** satıp aluu
to pay	**төлөө** tøløø
fine	**айып** ajıp
free	**бекер** beker
Where can I buy …?	**… каяктан сатып алсам болот?** … kajaktan satıp alsam bolot?
Is the bank open now?	**Банк азыр ачыкпы?** bank azır atʃıkpı?
When does it open?	**Ал канчада ачылат?** al kantʃada atʃılat?
When does it close?	**Ал канчага чейин иштейт?** al kantʃaga tʃejin iʃtejt?
How much?	**Канча турат?** kantʃa turat?
How much is this?	**Бул канча турат?** bul kantʃa turat?
That's too expensive.	**Бул аябай кымбат.** bul ajabaj kımbat.
Excuse me, where do I pay?	**Кечиресиз, касса кайсы жакта?** ketʃiresiz, kassa kajsı dʒakta?
Check, please.	**Эсептеп коюнузчу.** eseptep kojʉŋuztʃu.

Can I pay by credit card?

Карточка менен төлөсөм болобу?
kartotʃka menen tøløsøm bolobu?

Is there an ATM here?

Бул жерде банкомат барбы?
bul dʒerde bankomat barbɪ?

I'm looking for an ATM.

Мага банкомат керек эле.
maga bankomat kerek ele.

I'm looking for a foreign exchange office.

Мен акча алмаштыруу жайын издеп жаттым эле.
men aktʃa almaʃtıruu dʒajın izdep dʒattım ele.

I'd like to change …

Мен ... алмаштырайын дегем.
men ... almaʃtırajın degem.

What is the exchange rate?

Алмаштыруунун курсу кандай?
almaʃtıruunun kursu kandaj?

Do you need my passport?

Сизге менин паспортум керекпи?
sizge menin pasportum kerekpi?

Time

What time is it?	**Саат канча болду?** saat kantʃa boldu?
When?	**Качан?** katʃan?
At what time?	**Саат канчада?** saat kantʃada?
now | later | after …	**азыр | ананыраак | кийинчерээк …** azır | ananıraak | kijintʃereek …
one o'clock	**күндүзү саат бирде** kyndyzy saat birde
one fifteen	**бирден он беш мүнөт өткөндө** birden on beʃ mynøt øtkøndø
one thirty	**бир жарымда** bir dʒarımda
one forty-five	**экиге он беш мүнөт калганда** ekige on beʃ mynøt kalganda
one | two | three	**бир | эки | үч** bir | eki | ytʃ
four | five | six	**төрт | беш | алты** tørt | beʃ | altı
seven | eight | nine	**жети | сегиз | тогуз** dʒeti | segiz | toguz
ten | eleven | twelve	**он | он бир | он эки** on | on bir | on eki
in …	**… кийин** … kijin
five minutes	**беш мүнөт** beʃ mynøt
ten minutes	**он мүнөт** on mynøt
fifteen minutes	**он беш мүнөт** on beʃ mynøt
twenty minutes	**жыйырма мүнөт** dʒıjırma mynøt
half an hour	**жарым саат** dʒarım saat
an hour	**бир сааттан** bir saattan

in the morning	эртең менен
	erteŋ menen
early in the morning	таң эрте
	taŋ erte
this morning	бүгүн эртең менен
	bygyn erteŋ menen
tomorrow morning	эртең эртең менен
	erteŋ erteŋ menen

in the middle of the day	түштө
	tyʃtø
in the afternoon	түштөн кийин
	tyʃtøn kijin
in the evening	кечинде
	ketʃinde
tonight	бүгүн кечинде
	bygyn ketʃinde

at night	түндө
	tyndø
yesterday	кечээ
	ketʃee
today	бүгүн
	bygyn
tomorrow	эртең
	erteŋ
the day after tomorrow	бүрсүгүнү
	byrsygyny

What day is it today?	Бүгүн кайсы күн?
	bygyn kajsı kyn?
It's ...	Бүгүн ...
	bygyn ...
Monday	дүйшөмбү
	dyjʃømby
Tuesday	шейшемби
	ʃejʃembi
Wednesday	шаршемби
	ʃarʃembi

Thursday	бейшемби
	bejʃembi
Friday	жума
	dʒuma
Saturday	ишенби
	iʃenbi
Sunday	жекшемби
	dʒekʃembi

Greetings. Introductions

Hello.	**Саламатсызбы.** salamatsızbı.
Pleased to meet you.	**Сиз менен таанышканыбызга кубанычтамын.** siz menen taanıʃkanıbızga kubanıʧtamın.
Me too.	**Мен дагы.** men dagı.
I'd like you to meet ...	**Таанышып алгыла. Бул ...** taanıʃıp algıla. bul ...
Nice to meet you.	**Таанышканыбызга кубанычтамын.** taanıʃkanıbızga kubanıʧtamın.
How are you?	**Кандайсыз? Иштериңиз кандай?** kandajsız? iʃteriŋiz kandaj?
My name is ...	**Менин атым ...** menin atım ...
His name is ...	**Анын аты ...** anın atı ...
Her name is ...	**Анын аты ...** anın atı ...
What's your name?	**Сиздин атыңыз ким?** sizdin atıŋız kim?
What's his name?	**Анын аты ким?** anın atı kim?
What's her name?	**Анын аты ким?** anın atı kim?
What's your last name?	**Сиздин фамилияңыз кандай?** sizdin familijaŋız kandaj?
You can call me ...	**Мени ... десениз болот.** meni ... deseniz bolot.
Where are you from?	**Каяктан болосуз?** kajaktan bolosuz?
I'm from ...	**Мен ...** men ...
What do you do for a living?	**Сиз ким болуп иштейсиз?** siz kim bolup iʃtejsiz?
Who is this?	**Бул ким?** bul kim?
Who is he?	**Ал ким?** al kim?

Who is she? **Ал ким?**
al kim?

Who are they? **Алар кимдер?**
alar kimder?

This is … **Бул …**
bul …

my friend (masc.) **менин досум**
menin dosum

my friend (fem.) **менин курбум**
menin kurbum

my husband **менин күйөөм**
menin kyjøøm

my wife **менин аялым**
menin ajalım

---

my father **менин атам**
menin atam

my mother **менин апам**
menin apam

my brother **менин байкем**
menin bajkem

my sister **менин эжем**
menin edʒem

my son **менин уулум**
menin uulum

my daughter **менин кызым**
menin kızım

This is our son. **Бул биздин уулубуз.**
bul bizdin uulubuz.

This is our daughter. **Бул биздин кызыбыз.**
bul bizdin kızıbız.

These are my children. **Бул менин балдарым.**
bul menin baldarım.

These are our children. **Бул биздин балдарыбыз.**
bul bizdin baldarıbız.

Farewells

Good bye!	**Көрүшкөнчө!** køryʃkøntʃø!
Bye! (inform.)	**Жакшы бар!** dʒakʃı bar!

See you tomorrow.	**Эртеңкиге чейин.** erteŋkige tʃejin.
See you soon.	**Көрүшкөнгө чейин.** køryʃkøngø tʃejin.
See you at seven.	**Жетилерде жолугалы.** dʒetilerde dʒolugalı.

Have fun!	**Жакшы көңүл ачкыла!** dʒakʃı køŋyl atʃkıla!
Talk to you later.	**Ананыраак сүйлөшөлү.** ananıraak syjløʃøly.
Have a nice weekend.	**Эс алуу күндөр жакшы өтсүн.** es aluu kyndør dʒakʃı øtsyn.
Good night.	**Түнүң бейпил болсун.** tynyŋ bejpil bolsun.

It's time for me to go.	**Мен кетишим керек.** men ketiʃim kerek.
I have to go.	**Мен кетишим керек.** men ketiʃim kerek.
I will be right back.	**Мен азыр келем.** men azır kelem.

It's late.

Кеч болуп кетти.
ketʃ bolup ketti.

I have to get up early.

Мен эртең эрте турушум керек.
men erteŋ erte turuʃum kerek.

I'm leaving tomorrow.

Мен эртең кеткени жатам.
men erteŋ ketkeni dʒatam.

We're leaving tomorrow.

Биз эртең кеткени жатабыз.
biz erteŋ ketkeni dʒatabız.

Have a nice trip!

Жолуңар шыдыр болсун!
dʒoluŋar ʃıdır bolsun!

It was nice meeting you.

Сиз менен таанышканыма кубанычтамын.
siz menen taanıʃkanıma kubanıtʃtamın.

It was nice talking to you.

Сиз менен баарлашканыма кубанычтамын.
siz menen baarlaʃkanıma kubanıtʃtamın.

Thanks for everything.

Баардыгына рахмат.
baardıgına raχmat.

I had a very good time.

Мен убакытты сонун өткөрдүм.
men ubakıttı sonun øtkørdym.

We had a very good time.

Биз убакытты сонун өткөрдүк.
biz ubakıttı sonun øtkørdyk.

It was really great.

Баары ойдогудай болду.
baarı ojdogudaj boldu.

I'm going to miss you.

Мен сагынам.
men sagınam.

We're going to miss you.

Биз сагынабыз.
biz sagınabız.

Good luck!

Ийгилик!
ijgilik!

Say hi to ...

... салам айтып коюңуз.
... salam ajtıp kojuŋuz.

Foreign language

I don't understand.	**Мен түшүнбөй жатам.** men tyʃynbøj dʒatam.
Write it down, please.	**Жазып бериңизчи.** dʒazıp beriŋiztʃi.
Do you speak ...?	**Сиз ... сүйлөгөндү билесизби?** siz ... syjløgøndy bilesizbi?

I speak a little bit of ...	**Мен бир аз ... билем.** men bir az ... bilem.
English	**англисче** anglistʃe
Turkish	**түркчө** tyrktʃø
Arabic	**арабча** arabtʃa
French	**французча** frantsuztʃa

German	**немисче** nemistʃe
Italian	**италиялыкча** italijalıktʃa
Spanish	**испанча** ispantʃa
Portuguese	**португалча** portugaltʃa
Chinese	**кытайча** kıtajtʃa
Japanese	**японч о** japontʃo

Can you repeat that, please.	**Кайра кайталап коюңузчу.** kajra kajtalap kojuŋuztʃu.
I understand.	**Мен түшүнүп жатам.** men tyʃynyp dʒatam.
I don't understand.	**Мен түшүнбөй жатам.** men tyʃynbøj dʒatam.
Please speak more slowly.	**Жайыраак сүйлөңүзчү.** dʒajıraak syjløŋyztʃy.

Is that correct? (Am I saying it right?)	**Мындай туурабы?** mındaj tuurabı?
What is this? (What does this mean?)	**Бул эмне?** bul emne?

Apologies

Excuse me, please.	**Кечиресиз.** ketʃiresiz.
I'm sorry.	**Мен өкүнүп жатам.** men økynyp dʒatam.
I'm really sorry.	**Кечиресиз.** ketʃiresiz.
Sorry, it's my fault.	**Күнөөмдү мойнума алам.** **Күнөө менден кетти.** kynøømdy mojnuma alam. kynøø menden ketti.
My mistake.	**Менин жаңылыштыгым.** menin dʒaŋɯlɯʃtɯgɯm.
May I ...?	**Мен ... ?** men ... ?
Do you mind if I ...?	**Сиз каршы болбойсузбу,** **эгер мен ...?** siz karʃɯ bolbojsuzbu, eger men ...?
It's OK.	**Эчтеке болбойт.** etʃteke bolbojt.
It's all right.	**Баары жайында.** baarɯ dʒajɯnda.
Don't worry about it.	**Эч капачылык жок.** etʃ kapatʃɯlɯk dʒok.

Agreement

Yes.   **Ооба.**
                            ooba.

Yes, sure.   **Ооба, албетте.**
                            ooba, albette.

OK (Good!)   **Макул!**
                            makul!

Very well.   **Абдан жакшы.**
                            abdan dʒakʃı.

Certainly!   **Албетте!**
                            albette!

I agree.   **Мен макулмун.**
                            men makulmun.

That's correct.   **Чын.**
                            ʧın.

That's right.   **Туура.**
                            tuura.

You're right.   **Сиз туура айтасыз.**
                            siz tuura ajtasız.

I don't mind.   **Мен каршы эмесмин.**
                            men karʃı emesmin.

Absolutely right.   **Туптуура.**
                            tuptuura.

It's possible.   **Балким.**
                            balkim.

That's a good idea.   **Бул жакшы.**
                            bul dʒakʃı.

I can't say no.   **Жок дей албайм.**
                            dʒok dey albajm.

I'd be happy to.   **Кубанычтамын.**
                            kubanıʧtamın.

With pleasure.   **Чын көңүлүм менен.**
                            ʧın køŋylym menen.

Refusal. Expressing doubt

No.
Жок.
dʒok.

Certainly not.
Албетте жок.
albette dʒok.

I don't agree.
Мен макул эмесмин.
men makul emesmin.

I don't think so.
Мен антип ойлобойм.
men antip ojlobojm.

It's not true.
Ишенбейм.
iʃenbejm.

You are wrong.
Сиз туура эмес сүйлөп жатасыз.
siz tuura emes syjløp dʒatasız.

I think you are wrong.
Менин оюмча, сиз жаңылышып жатасыз.
menin odʒumtʃa, siz dʒaŋılıʃıp dʒatasız.

I'm not sure.
Билбейм, так айталбайм.
bilbejm, tak ajtalbajm.

It's impossible.
Мындай мүмкүн эмес.
mındaj mymkyn emes.

Nothing of the kind (sort)!
Болбогон кеп!
bolbogon kep!

The exact opposite.
Тескерисинче!
teskerisintʃe!

I'm against it.
Мен каршымын.
men karʃımın.

I don't care.
Мага баары бир.
maga baarı bir.

I have no idea.
Билбейм.
bilbejm.

I doubt it.
Ушундай экенине күмөнүм бар.
uʃundaj ekenine kymønym bar.

Sorry, I can't.
Кечиресиз, бирок мен анте албайм.
ketʃiresiz, birok men ante albajm.

Sorry, I don't want to.
Кечиресиз, мен каалаган жокмун.
ketʃiresiz, men kaalagan dʒokmun.

Thank you, but I don't need this.
Рахмат, мунун мага кереги жок.
raχmat, munun maga keregi dʒok.

It's getting late.
Кеч болуп кетти.
ketʃ bolup ketti.

I have to get up early.

Мен эртең эрте турушум керек.
men erteŋ erte turuſum kerek.

I don't feel well.

Мен өзүмдү жаман сезип жатам.
men øzymdy dʒaman sezip dʒatam.

Expressing gratitude

Thank you.	**Рахмат.** raχmat.
Thank you very much.	**Чоң рахмат.** ʧoŋ raχmat.
I really appreciate it.	**Чоң рахмат.** ʧoŋ raχmat.
I'm really grateful to you.	**Мен сизге ыраазымын.** men sizge ıraazımın.
We are really grateful to you.	**Биз сизге ыраазыбыз.** biz sizge ıraazıbız.

Thank you for your time.	**Убакыт бөлгөнүңүз үчүн рахмат.** ubakıt bølgønyŋyz yʧyn raχmat.
Thanks for everything.	**Баардыгына рахмат.** baardıgına raχmat.
Thank you for …	**… рахмат.** … raχmat.
your help	**сиздин жардам бергениңиз үчүн** sizdin dʒardam bergeniŋiz yʧyn
a nice time	**жакшы өткөргөн убакыт үчүн** dʒakʃı øtkørgøn ubakıt yʧyn

a wonderful meal	**даамдуу тамак үчүн** daamduu tamak yʧyn
a pleasant evening	**жагымдуу кече үчүн** dʒagımduu keʧe yʧyn
a wonderful day	**сонун күн үчүн** sonun kyn yʧyn
an amazing journey	**кызыктуу саякат үчүн** kızıktuu sajakat yʧyn

Don't mention it.	**Эчтеке эмес.** eʧteke emes.
You are welcome.	**Рахмат айтуунун кажети жок.** raχmat ajtuunun kadʒeti dʒok.
Any time.	**Ар дайым даярмын.** ar dajım dajarmın.
My pleasure.	**Жардам бергенге кубанычтамын.** dʒardam bergenge kubanıʧtamın.
Forget it.	**Жөн коюңуз. Баары жайында** dʒøn kodʒuŋuz. baarı dʒajında
Don't worry about it.	**Эч капачылык жок.** eʧ kapaʧılık dʒok.

Congratulations. Best wishes

Congratulations!	**Куттуктайм!** kuttuktajm!
Happy birthday!	**Туулган күнүң менен!** tuulgan kynyŋ menen!
Merry Christmas!	**Рождество көңүлдүү өтсүн!** rodʒdestvo køŋyldyy øtsyn!
Happy New Year!	**Жаңы жылыңыздар менен!** dʒaŋı dʒılıŋızdar menen!
Happy Easter!	**Пасха майрамыңар менен!** pasχa majramıŋar menen!
Happy Hanukkah!	**Ханука майрамыңыздар кут болсун!** χanuka majramıŋızdar kut bolsun!
Cheers!	**Сиздин ден-соолугуңуз үчүн!** sizdin den-sooluguŋuz yʧyn!
Let's drink to …!	**… үчүн алып жиберели!** … yʧyn alıp dʒibereli!
To our success!	**Биздин ийгилигибиз үчүн!** bizdin ijgiligibiz yʧyn!
To your success!	**Сиздин ийгилигиңиз үчүн!** sizdin ijgiliginiz yʧyn!
Good luck!	**Ийгилик!** ijgilik!
Have a nice day!	**Күнүңүз куунак өтсүн!** kynyŋyz kuunak øtsyn!
Have a good holiday!	**Дем алуу күндөрүңүз жакшы өтсүн!** dem aluu kyndøryŋyz dʒakʃı øtsyn!
Have a safe journey!	**Жолуңуз шыдыр болсун!** dʒoluŋuz ʃıdır bolsun!
I hope you get better soon!	**Эртерээк сакайып кетишиңизди каалайм.** ertereek sakayıp ketiʃiŋizdi kaalajm.

Socializing

Why are you sad?	**Эмнеге көңүлүңүз жок?** emnege køŋylyŋyz dʒok?
Smile! Cheer up!	**Күлүп коюңузчу!** kylyp kojuŋuztʃu!
Are you free tonight?	**Сиз бүгүн кечинде бошсузбу?** siz bygyn ketʃinde boʃsuzbu?

May I offer you a drink?	**Мен сизге ичимдик сунуш кылсам болобу?** men sizge itʃimdik sunuʃ kılsam bolobu?
Would you like to dance?	**Бийлегиңиз келген жокпу?** bijleginiz kelgen dʒokpu?
Let's go to the movies.	**Балким киного барып келбейлиби?** balkim kinogo barıp kelbejlibi?

May I invite you to …?	**Мен сизди … чакырсам болобу?** men sizdi … tʃakırsam bolobu?
a restaurant	**ресторанга** restoranga
the movies	**киного** kinogo
the theater	**театрга** teatrga
go for a walk	**сейилдөөгө** sejildøøgø

At what time?	**Саат канчада?** saat kantʃada?
tonight	**бүгүн кечинде** bygyn ketʃinde
at six	**саат алтыда** saat altıda
at seven	**саат жетиде** saat dʒetide
at eight	**саат сегизде** saat segizde
at nine	**саат тогузда** saat toguzda

Do you like it here?	**Сизге бул жер жактыбы?** sizge bul dʒer dʒaktıbı?
Are you here with someone?	**Сиз бул жерде бирөө мененсизби?** siz bul dʒerde birøø menensizbi?

I'm with my friend.	**Мен досум /кызым/ мененмин.** men dosum /kızım/ menenmin.
I'm with my friends.	**Мен досторум мененмин.** men dostorum menenmin.
No, I'm alone.	**Мен жалгызмын.** men dʒalgızmın.
Do you have a boyfriend?	**Сенин сүйлөшкөн жигитиң барбы?** senin syjløʃkøn dʒigitiŋ barbı?
I have a boyfriend.	**Менин досум бар.** menin dosum bar.
Do you have a girlfriend?	**Сенин курбуң барбы?** senin kurbuŋ barbı?
I have a girlfriend.	**Менин сүйлөшкөн кызым бар.** menin syjløʃkøn kızım bar.
Can I see you again?	**Биз дагы жолугабызбы?** biz dagı dʒolugabızbı?
Can I call you?	**Мен сага чалсам болобу?** men saga tʃalsam bolobu?
Call me. (Give me a call.)	**Мага чалчы.** maga tʃaltʃı.
What's your number?	**Сенин телефон номериң кандай?** senin telefon nomeriŋ kandaj?
I miss you.	**Мен сени сагынып жатам.** men seni sagınıp dʒatam.
You have a beautiful name.	**Атыңыз кандай сонун.** atıŋız kandaj sonun.
I love you.	**Мен сени сүйөм.** men seni syjøm.
Will you marry me?	**Мага турмушка чыгасыңбы?** maga turmuʃka tʃıgasıŋbı?
You're kidding!	**Коюңузчу!** kojuŋuztʃu?
I'm just kidding.	**Мен жөн эле тамашалап жатам.** men dʒøn ele tamaʃalap dʒatam.
Are you serious?	**Сиз чын эле айтып жатасызбы?** siz tʃın ele ajtıp dʒatasızbı?
I'm serious.	**Мен чын айтып жатам.** men tʃın ajtıp dʒatam.
Really?!	**Чын элеби?!** tʃın elebi?!
It's unbelievable!	**Мындай мүмкүн эмес.** mındaj mymkyn emes.
I don't believe you.	**Мен сизге ишенбейм.** men sizge iʃenbejm.
I can't.	**Мен анте албайм.** men ante albajm.
I don't know.	**Мен билбейм.** men bilbejm.

I don't understand you.	**Сизди түшүнбөй турам.**
	sizdi tyʃynbøj turam.
Please go away.	**Кетиңизчи, суранам.**
	ketiŋizʧi, suranam.
Leave me alone!	**Мени өз жайыма койгулачы.**
	meni øz dʒajıma kojgulaʧı.

I can't stand him.	**Мен аны көргүм келбейт.**
	men anı kørgym kelbejt.
You are disgusting!	**Сизди көрөйүн деген көзүм жок!**
	sizdi kørøjyn degen køzym dʒok!
I'll call the police!	**Мен милицияны чакырам!**
	men militsijanı ʧakıram!

Sharing impressions. Emotions

I like it.	**Мага бул жакты.** maga bul dʒaktı.
Very nice.	**Жакшынакай экен.** dʒakʃınakaj eken.
That's great!	**Сонун экен!** sonun eken!
It's not bad.	**Жаман эмес.** dʒaman emes.
I don't like it.	**Мага бул жаккан жок.** maga bul dʒakkan dʒok.
It's not good.	**Бул жакшы эмес.** bul dʒakʃı emes.
It's bad.	**Бул жаман.** bul dʒaman.
It's very bad.	**Бул аябай жаман.** bul ajabaj dʒaman.
It's disgusting.	**Көңүлдү иренжиткен нерсе экен.** køŋyldy irendʒitken nerse eken.
I'm happy.	**Бактылуумун.** baktıluumun.
I'm content.	**Ыраазымын.** iraazımın.
I'm in love.	**Сүйүп калдым.** syjyp kaldım.
I'm calm.	**Тынч элемин.** tıntʃ elemin.
I'm bored.	**Зеригип жатам.** zerigip dʒatam.
I'm tired.	**Мен чарчадым.** men tʃartʃadım.
I'm sad.	**Көңүлүм болбой жатат.** køŋylym bolboj dʒatat.
I'm frightened.	**Жүрөгүм түшүп жатат.** dʒyrøgym tyʃyp dʒatat.
I'm angry.	**Жиним келип жатат.** dʒinim kelip dʒatat.
I'm worried.	**Тынчым кетип жатат.** tıntʃım ketip dʒatat.
I'm nervous.	**Нервим кайнап турат.** nervim kajnap turat.

I'm jealous. (envious)

Ичим күйүп жатат.
itʃim kyjyp dʒatat.

I'm surprised.

Таң калыштуу.
taŋ kalıʃtuu.

I'm perplexed.

Мен эмне дээримди билбей жатам.
men emne deerimdi bilbej dʒatam.

Problems. Accidents

I've got a problem.	**Менде көйгөй чыкты.** mende køygøj ʧıktı.
We've got a problem.	**Бизде көйгөй чыкты.** bizde køjgøj ʧıktı.
I'm lost.	**Мен адашып кеттим.** men adaʃıp kettim.
I missed the last bus (train).	**Мен акыркы автобуска жетишпей калдым.** men akırkı avtobuska ʤetiʃpej kaldım.
I don't have any money left.	**Менин таптакыр акчам жок калды.** menin taptakır akʧam ʤok kaldı.

I've lost my ...	**Мен ... жоготуп алдым.** men ... ʤogotup aldım.
Someone stole my ...	**Мен ... уурдатып ийдим.** men ... uurdatıp ijdim.
passport	**паспортумду** pasportumdu
wallet	**капчыгымды** kapʧıgımdı
papers	**документтеримди** dokumentterimdi
ticket	**билетимди** biletimdi

money	**акчамды** akʧamdı
handbag	**сумкамды** sumkamdı
camera	**фотоаппаратымды** fotoapparatımdı
laptop	**ноутбугумду** noutbugumdu
tablet computer	**планшетимди** planʃetimdi
mobile phone	**телефонумду** telefonumdu

Help me!	**Жардамга!** ʤardamga!
What's happened?	**Эмне болду?** emne boldu?

fire	**өрт** ørt
shooting	**атышуу** atıʃuu
murder	**өлтүрүү** øltyryy
explosion	**жарылуу** dʒarıluu
fight	**мушташ** muʃtaʃ

Call the police!	**Милицияны чакырып коюңузчу!** militsijanı tʃakırıp kojʉŋuztʃu!
Please hurry up!	**Тезирээк, сураныч!** tezireek, suranıtʃ!
I'm looking for the police station.	**Мен милиция бөлүмүн издеп жаттым эле.** men militsija bølymyn izdep dʒattım ele.
I need to make a call.	**Мен чалышым керек.** men tʃalıʃım kerek.
May I use your phone?	**Телефон чалып алсам болобу?** telefon tʃalıp alsam bolobu?

I've been …	**Мени …** meni …
mugged	**тоноп кетишти** tonop ketiʃti
robbed	**мен уурдатып ийдим.** men uurdatıp ijdim.
raped	**зордуктап кетишти** zorduktap ketiʃti
attacked (beaten up)	**сабап кетишти.** sabap ketiʃti.

Are you all right?	**Баары жайындабы?** baarı dʒajındabı?
Did you see who it was?	**Ким экенин сиз көрдүңүзбү?** kim ekenin siz kørdyŋyzby?
Would you be able to recognize the person?	**Сиз аны тааный аласызбы?** siz anı taanıj alasızbı?
Are you sure?	**Аны так айта аласызбы?** anı tak ajta alasızbı?

Please calm down.	**Суранам, тынчтансаңыз.** suranam, tıntʃtansaŋız.
Take it easy!	**Жайыраак!** dʒajıraak!
Don't worry!	**Кам санабаңыз.** kam sanabaŋız.
Everything will be fine.	**Баары жакшы болот.** baarı dʒakʃı bolot.

Everything's all right.

Баары жайында.
baarı ʤajında.

Come here, please.

Бери келсеңиз.
beri kelseŋiz.

I have some questions for you.

Мен сизге бир нече суроом бар.
men sizge bir neʧe suroom bar.

Wait a moment, please.

Күтүп турсаңыз.
kytyp tursaŋız.

Do you have any I.D.?

Сиздин документтериңиз барбы?
sizdin dokumentteriŋiz barbı?

Thanks. You can leave now.

Рахмат. Сиз бара берсеңиз болот.
raχmat. siz bara berseŋiz bolot.

Hands behind your head!

Колуңузду башыңызга алыңыз!
koluŋuzdu baʃıŋızga alıŋız!

You're under arrest!

Сиз камакка алындыңыз!
siz kamakka alındıŋız!

Health problems

Please help me.	**Мага жардам берип коюнузчу.** maga dʒardam berip kodʒuŋuztʃu.
I don't feel well.	**Мен өзүмдү жаман сезип жатам.** men øzymdy dʒaman sezip dʒatam.
My husband doesn't feel well.	**Менин күйөөм өзүн жаман сезип жатат.** menin kyjøøm øzyn dʒaman sezip dʒatat.
My son ...	**Менин балам ...** menin balam ...
My father ...	**Менин атам ...** menin atam ...
My wife doesn't feel well.	**Менин аялым өзүн жаман сезип жатат.** menin ajalım øzyn dʒaman sezip jatat.
My daughter ...	**Менин кызым ...** menin kızım ...
My mother ...	**Менин апам ...** menin apam ...
I've got a ...	**Менин ... ооруп жатат.** menin ... oorup dʒatat.
headache	**башым** baʃım
sore throat	**тамагым** tamagım
stomach ache	**ичим** itʃim
toothache	**тишим** tiʃim
I feel dizzy.	**Менин башым айланып жатат.** menin baʃım ajlanıp dʒatat.
He has a fever.	**Анын дене табы көтөрүлүп жатат.** anın dene tabı køtørylyp dʒatat.
She has a fever.	**Анын дене табы көтөрүлүп жатат.** anın dene tabı køtørylyp dʒatat.
I can't breathe.	**Мен дем алалбай жатам.** men dem alalbaj dʒatam.
I'm short of breath.	**Мага дем жетпей жатат.** maga dem dʒetpej dʒatat.

I am asthmatic.	**Менин астмам бар.** menin astmam bar.
I am diabetic.	**Менин диабетим бар.** menin diabetim bar.
I can't sleep.	**Менин уйкум качып жатат.** menin ujkum katʃïp dʒatat.
food poisoning	**тамак-ашка уулануу** tamak-aʃka uulanuu

It hurts here.	**Мобу жерим ооруп жатат.** mobu dʒerim oorup dʒatat.
Help me!	**Жардамга!** dʒardamga!
I am here!	**Мен бул жердемин!** men bul dʒerdemin!
We are here!	**Биз бул жердебиз!** biz bul dʒerdebiz!
Get me out of here!	**Мени чыгаргылачы!** meni tʃïgargïlatʃï!

I need a doctor.	**Мага доктур керек эле.** maga doktur kerek ele.
I can't move.	**Мен кыймылдай албай жатам.** men kïjmïldaj albaj dʒatam.
I can't move my legs.	**Мен бутумду сезбей жатам.** men butumdu sezbej dʒatam.

I have a wound.	**Мен жарадармын.** men dʒaradarmïn.
Is it serious?	**Абалым аябай эле начарбы?** abalïm ajabaj ele natʃarbï?
My documents are in my pocket.	**Менин документтерим чөнтөгүмдө.** menin dokumentterim tʃөntөgymdө.

Calm down!	**Тынчтансаңыз!** tïntʃtansaŋïz!
May I use your phone?	**Телефон чалып алсам болобу?** telefon tʃalïp alsam bolobu?

Call an ambulance!	**Тез жардамды чакырып коюңузчу!** tez dʒardamdï tʃakïrïp kodʒuŋuztʃu!
It's urgent!	**Тезирээк!** tezireek!
It's an emergency!	**Тезирээк керек!** tezireek kerek!
Please hurry up!	**Тезирээк, сураныч!** tezireek, suranïtʃ!

Would you please call a doctor?	**Доктурду чакырып коюңузчу.** dokturdu tʃakïrïp kojuŋuztʃu.
Where is the hospital?	**Айтып коюңузчу, оорукана каякта?** ajtïp kojuŋuztʃu, oorukana kajakta?

How are you feeling?

Сиз өзүнүздү кандай сезип жатасыз?
siz özyŋyzdy kandaj sezip dʒatasız?

Are you all right?

Баары жайындабы?
baarı dʒajındabı?

What's happened?

Эмне болду?
emne boldu?

I feel better now.

Мен өзүмдү жакшы сезип калдым.
men özymdy dʒakʃı sezip kaldım.

It's OK.

Баары жайында.
baarı dʒajında.

It's all right.

Баары жакшы.
baarı dʒakʃı.

At the pharmacy

pharmacy (drugstore)	**дарыкана** darıkana
24-hour pharmacy	**күнү-түнү иштеген дарыкана** kyny-tyny iʃtegen darıkana
Where is the closest pharmacy?	**Жакын жерде дарыкана барбы?** dʒakın dʒerde darıkana barbı?
Is it open now?	**Азыр ал жак ачыкпы?** azır al dʒak atʃıkpı?
At what time does it open?	**Саат канчада ал жак ачылат?** saat kantʃada al dʒak atʃılat?
At what time does it close?	**Ал жак саат канчага чейин иштейт?** al dʒak saat kantʃaga tʃejin iʃtejt?
Is it far?	**Бул жерден алыспы?** bul dʒerden alıspı?
Can I get there on foot?	**Мен ал жакка жөө жете аламбы?** men al dʒakka dʒøø dʒete alambı?
Can you show me on the map?	**Ал жакты картадан көрсөтүп бериңизчи.** al dʒaktı kartadan kørsøtyp beriŋiztʃi.
Please give me something for …	**Мага … дарысын берип коёсузбу** maga … darısın berip kojosuzbu
a headache	**баш оорунун** baʃ oorunun
a cough	**жөтөлдүн** dʒøtøldyn
a cold	**суук тийгендин** suuk tijgendin
the flu	**сасык тумоонун** sasık tumoonun
a fever	**дененин табын түшүрүүчү** denenin tabın tyʃyryytʃy
a stomach ache	**ич оорунун** itʃ oorunun
nausea	**жүрөк айлануунун** dʒyrøk ajlanuunun
diarrhea	**ич өткөндүн** itʃ øtkøndyn
constipation	**ич катуунун** itʃ katuunun

pain in the back	**белим ооруп жатат** belim oorup dʒatat
chest pain	**төшүм ооруп жатат** tøʃym oorup dʒatat
side stitch	**каптал жагым ооруп жатат** kaptal dʒagım oorup dʒatat
abdominal pain	**ичим ооруп жатат** itʃim oorup dʒatat

pill	**дары** darı
ointment, cream	**май** maj
syrup	**сироп** sirop
spray	**чачыратма** tʃatʃıratma
drops	**тамчылатма** tamtʃılatma

You need to go to the hospital.	**Сизге ооруканага баруу керек.** sizge oorukanaga baruu kerek.
health insurance	**камсыздандыруу күбөлүгү** kamsızdandıruu kybølygy
prescription	**рецепт** retsept
insect repellant	**курт-кумурскалардан сактоо каражаты** kurt-kumurskalardan saktoo karadʒatı
Band Aid	**лейкопластырь** lejkoplastırі

The bare minimum

Excuse me, ... | **Кечиресиз, ...**
ketʃiresiz, ...

Hello. | **Саламатсызбы.**
salamatsızbı.

Thank you. | **Рахмат.**
raχmat.

Good bye. | **Көрүшкөнчө.**
køryʃkøntʃø.

Yes. | **Ооба.**
ooba.

No. | **Жок.**
dʒok.

I don't know. | **Мен билбейм.**
men bilbejm.

Where? | Where to? | When? | **Каякта? | Каякка? | Качан?**
kajakta? | kajakka? | katʃan?

I need ... | **Мага ... керек эле.**
maga ... kerek ele.

I want ... | **Мен ... гым келет.**
men ... gım kelet.

Do you have ...? | **Силерде ... барбы?**
silerde ... barbı?

Is there a ... here? | **Бул жерде ... барбы?**
bul dʒerde ... barbı?

May I ...? | **Мага ... болобу?**
maga ... bolobu?

..., please (polite request) | **Сураныч**
suranıtʃ

I'm looking for ... | **Мен ... издеп жаттым эле.**
men ... izdep dʒattım ele.

the restroom | **даараткана**
daaratkana

an ATM | **банкомат**
bankomat

a pharmacy (drugstore) | **дарыкана**
darıkana

a hospital | **оорукана**
oorukana

the police station | **милиция бөлүмү**
militsija bølymy

the subway | **метро**
metro

a taxi	**такси**
	taksi
the train station	**вокзал**
	vokzal

My name is ...	**Менин атым ...**
	menin atım ...
What's your name?	**Сиздин атыңыз ким?**
	sizdin atıŋız kim?
Could you please help me?	**Мага жардам берип коюңузчу.**
	maga dʒardam berip kodʒuŋuztʃu.
I've got a problem.	**Менде көйгөй чыкты.**
	mende køygøj tʃıktı.
I don't feel well.	**Мен өзүмдү жаман сезип жатам.**
	men øzymdy dʒaman sezip dʒatam.
Call an ambulance!	**Тез жардамды чакырып коюңузчу!**
	tez dʒardamdı tʃakırıp kodʒuŋuztʃu!
May I make a call?	**Телефон чалып алсам болобу?**
	telefon tʃalıp alsam bolobu?

I'm sorry.	**Кечирип коюңуз**
	ketʃirip kojuŋuz
You're welcome.	**Эчтеке эмес**
	etʃteke emes

I, me	**мен**
	men
you (inform.)	**сен**
	sen
he	**ал**
	al
she	**ал**
	al
they (masc.)	**алар**
	alar
they (fem.)	**алар**
	alar
we	**биз**
	biz
you (pl)	**сиз**
	siz
you (sg, form.)	**Сиз**
	siz

ENTRANCE	**КИРҮҮ**
	kiryy
EXIT	**ЧЫГУУ**
	tʃıguu
OUT OF ORDER	**ИШТЕБЕЙТ**
	iʃtebejt
CLOSED	**ЖАБЫК**
	dʒabık

OPEN	**АЧЫК** atʃık
FOR WOMEN	**АЙЫМДАР ҮЧҮН** ajımdar ytʃyn
FOR MEN	**ЭРКЕКТЕР ҮЧҮН** erkekter ytʃyn

CONCISE
DICTIONARY

This section contains more
than 1,500 useful words
arranged alphabetically.
The dictionary includes a lot
of gastronomic terms and
will be helpful when ordering
food at a restaurant or buying
groceries

T&P Books Publishing

DICTIONARY CONTENTS

1. Time. Calendar	76
2. Numbers. Numerals	77
3. Humans. Family	78
4. Human body	79
5. Medicine. Diseases. Drugs	81
6. Feelings. Emotions. Conversation	82
7. Clothing. Personal accessories	83
8. City. Urban institutions	85
9. Money. Finances	86
10. Transportation	87
11. Food. Part 1	88
12. Food. Part 2	90
13. House. Apartment. Part 1	91
14. House. Apartment. Part 2	92
15. Professions. Social status	93
16. Sport	95

T&P Books Publishing

17. Foreign languages. Orthography 96

18. The Earth. Geography 97

19. Countries of the world. Part 1 98

20. Countries of the world. Part 2 100

21. Weather. Natural disasters 101

22. Animals. Part 1 102

23. Animals. Part 2 103

24. Trees. Plants 105

25. Various useful words 106

26. Modifiers. Adjectives. Part 1 107

27. Modifiers. Adjectives. Part 2 108

28. Verbs. Part 1 109

29. Verbs. Part 2 111

30. Verbs. Part 3 112

T&P Books Publishing

time	убакыт	ubakıt
hour	саат	saat
half an hour	жарым саат	dʒarım saat
minute	мүнөт	mynøt
second	секунда	sekunda
today (adv)	бүгүн	bygyn
tomorrow (adv)	эртең	erteŋ
yesterday (adv)	кечээ	ketʃee
Monday	дүйшөмбү	dyjʃømby
Tuesday	шейшемби	ʃejʃembi
Wednesday	шаршемби	ʃarʃembi
Thursday	бейшемби	bejʃembi
Friday	жума	dʒuma
Saturday	ишенби	iʃenbi
Sunday	жекшемби	dʒekʃembi
day	күн	kyn
working day	иш күнү	iʃ kyny
public holiday	майрам күнү	majram kyny
weekend	дем алыш күндөр	dem alıʃ kyndør
week	жума	dʒuma
last week (adv)	өткөн жумада	øtkøn dʒumada
next week (adv)	келаткан жумада	kelatkan dʒumada
sunrise	күндүн чыгышы	kyndyn tʃıgıʃı
sunset	күн батуу	kyn batuu
in the morning	эртең менен	erteŋ menen
in the afternoon	түштөн кийин	tyʃtøn kijin
in the evening	кечинде	ketʃinde
tonight (this evening)	бүгүн кечинде	bygyn ketʃinde
at night	түндө	tyndø
midnight	жарым түн	dʒarım tyn
January	январь	janvarʲ
February	февраль	fevralʲ
March	март	mart
April	апрель	aprelʲ
May	май	maj
June	июнь	ijʉnʲ

July	июль	ijɯlʲ
August	август	avgust
September	сентябрь	sentʲabrʲ
October	октябрь	oktʲabrʲ
November	ноябрь	nojabrʲ
December	декабрь	dekabrʲ

in spring	жазында	dʒazɯnda
in summer	жайында	dʒajɯnda
in fall	күзүндө	kyzyndø
in winter	кышында	kɯʃɯnda

month	ай	aj
season (summer, etc.)	мезгил	mezgil
year	жыл	dʒɯl
century	кылым	kɯlɯm

2. Numbers. Numerals

digit, figure	санарип	sanarip
number	сан	san
minus sign	кемитүү	kemityy
plus sign	плюс	plʉs
sum, total	жыйынтык	dʒɯjɯntɯk

first (adj)	биринчи	birintʃi
second (adj)	экинчи	ekintʃi
third (adj)	үчүнчү	ytʃyntʃy

0 zero	нөл	nøl
1 one	бир	bir
2 two	эки	eki
3 three	үч	ytʃ
4 four	төрт	tørt

5 five	беш	beʃ
6 six	алты	altɯ
7 seven	жети	dʒeti
8 eight	сегиз	segiz
9 nine	тогуз	toguz
10 ten	он	on

11 eleven	он бир	on bir
12 twelve	он эки	on eki
13 thirteen	он үч	on ytʃ
14 fourteen	он төрт	on tørt
15 fifteen	он беш	on beʃ

| 16 sixteen | он алты | on altɯ |
| 17 seventeen | он жети | on dʒeti |

| 18 eighteen | он сегиз | on segiz |
| 19 nineteen | он тогуз | on toguz |

20 twenty	жыйырма	dʒıjırma
30 thirty	отуз	otuz
40 forty	кырк	kırk
50 fifty	элүү	elyy

60 sixty	алтымыш	altımıʃ
70 seventy	жетимиш	dʒetimiʃ
80 eighty	сексен	seksen
90 ninety	токсон	tokson

100 one hundred	бир жүз	bir dʒyz
200 two hundred	эки жүз	eki dʒyz
300 three hundred	үч жүз	ytʃ dʒyz
400 four hundred	төрт жүз	tørt dʒyz
500 five hundred	беш жүз	beʃ dʒyz

600 six hundred	алты жүз	altı dʒyz
700 seven hundred	жети жүз	dʒeti dʒyz
800 eight hundred	сегиз жүз	segiz dʒyz
900 nine hundred	тогуз жүз	toguz dʒyz
1000 one thousand	бир миң	bir miŋ

| 10000 ten thousand | он миң | on miŋ |
| one hundred thousand | жүз миң | dʒyz miŋ |

| million | миллион | million |
| billion | миллиард | milliard |

3. Humans. Family

man (adult male)	эркек	erkek
young man	улан	ulan
teenager	өспүрүм	øspyrym
woman	аял	ajal
girl (young woman)	кыз	kız

age	жаш	dʒaʃ
adult (adj)	чоң киши	tʃoŋ kiʃi
middle-aged (adj)	орто жаш	orto dʒaʃ
elderly (adj)	жашап калган	dʒaʃap kalgan
old (adj)	картаң	kartaŋ

old man	абышка	abıʃka
old woman	кемпир	kempir
retirement	бааракы	baarakı
to retire (from job)	ардактуу эс алууга чыгуу	ardaktuu es aluuga tʃıguu

retiree	бааргер	baarger
mother	эне	ene
father	ата	ata
son	уул	uul
daughter	кыз	kız
brother	бир тууган	bir tuugan
elder brother	байке	bajke
younger brother	ини	ini
sister	бир тууган	bir tuugan
elder sister	эже	edʒe
younger sister	синди	siŋdi
parents	ата-эне	ata-ene
child	бала	bala
children	балдар	baldar
stepmother	өгөй эне	øgøj ene
stepfather	өгөй ата	øgøj ata
grandmother	чоң апа	ʧoŋ apa
grandfather	чоң ата	ʧoŋ ata
grandson	небере бала	nebere bala
granddaughter	небере кыз	nebere kız
grandchildren	неб релер	nebereler
uncle	таяке	tajake
aunt	таяже	tajadʒe
nephew	ини	ini
niece	жээн	dʒeen
wife	аял	ajal
husband	эр	er
married (masc.)	аялы бар	ajalı bar
married (fem.)	күйөөдө	kyjøødø
widow	жесир	dʒesir
widower	жесир	dʒesir
name (first name)	аты	atı
surname (last name)	фамилиясы	familijası
relative	тууган	tuugan
friend (masc.)	дос	dos
friendship	достук	dostuk
partner	өнөктөш	ønøktøʃ
superior (n)	башчы	baʃʧı
colleague	кесиптеш	kesipteʃ
neighbors	кошуналар	koʃunalar

4. Human body

organism (body)	организм	organizm
body	дене	dene

heart	жүрөк	dʒyrøk
blood	кан	kan
brain	мээ	mee
nerve	нерв	nerv
bone	сөөк	søøk
skeleton	скелет	skelet
spine (backbone)	кыр арка	kır arka
rib	кабырга	kabırga
skull	баш сөөгү	baʃ søøgy
muscle	булчуң	bultʃuŋ
lungs	өпкө	øpkø
skin	тери	teri
head	баш	baʃ
face	бет	bet
nose	мурун	murun
forehead	чеке	tʃeke
cheek	бет	bet
mouth	ооз	ooz
tongue	тил	til
tooth	тиш	tiʃ
lips	эриндер	erinder
chin	ээк	eek
ear	кулак	kulak
neck	моюн	mojʉn
throat	тамак	tamak
eye	көз	køz
pupil	карек	karek
eyebrow	каш	kaʃ
eyelash	кирпик	kirpik
hair	чач	tʃatʃ
hairstyle	чач жасоо	tʃatʃ dʒasoo
mustache	мурут	murut
beard	сакал	sakal
to have (a beard, etc.)	мурут коюу	murut kojʉu
bald (adj)	таз	taz
hand	беш манжа	beʃ mandʒa
arm	кол	kol
finger	манжа	mandʒa
nail	тырмак	tırmak
palm	алакан	alakan
shoulder	ийин	ijin
leg	бут	but
foot	таман	taman

knee	тизе	tize
heel	согончок	sogontʃok
back	арка жон	arka dʒon
waist	бел	bel
beauty mark	мең	meŋ
birthmark	кал	kal
(café au lait spot)		

5. Medicine. Diseases. Drugs

health	ден-соолук	den-sooluk
well (not sick)	дени сак	deni sak
sickness	ооруу	ooru
to be sick	ооруу	ooruu
ill, sick (adj)	оорулуу	ooruluu
cold (illness)	суук тийүү	suuk tijyy
to catch a cold	суук тийгизип алуу	suuk tijgizip aluu
tonsillitis	ангина	angina
pneumonia	кабыргадан сезгенүү	kabırgadan sezgenyy
flu, influenza	сасык тумоо	sasık tumoo
runny nose (coryza)	мурдунан суу агуу	murdunan suu aguu
cough	жөтөл	dʒøtøl
to cough (vi)	жөтөлүү	dʒøtølyy
to sneeze (vi)	чүчкүрүү	tʃytʃkyryy
stroke	мээге кан куюлуу	meege kan kujʉluu
heart attack	инфаркт	infarkt
allergy	аллергия	allergija
asthma	астма	astma
diabetes	диабет	diabet
tumor	шишик	ʃiʃik
cancer	рак	rak
alcoholism	аракечтик	araketʃtik
AIDS	СПИД	spid
fever	безгек	bezgek
seasickness	деңиз оорусу	deŋiz oorusu
bruise (hématome)	көк-ала	køk-ala
bump (lump)	шишик	ʃiʃik
to limp (vi)	аксоо	aksoo
dislocation	муундун чыгып кетүүсү	muundun tʃıgıp ketyysy
to dislocate (vt)	чыгарып алуу	tʃıgarıp aluu
fracture	сынуу	sınuu
burn (injury)	күйүк	kyjyk
injury	кокустатып алуу	kokustatıp aluu

| pain, ache | оору | ooru |
| toothache | тиш оорусу | tiʃ oorusu |

to sweat (perspire)	тердөө	terdøø
deaf (adj)	дүлөй	dyløj
mute (adj)	дудук	duduk

immunity	иммунитет	immunitet
virus	вирус	virus
microbe	микроб	mikrob
bacterium	бактерия	bakterija
infection	жугуштуу илдет	dʒuguʃtuu ildet

hospital	оорукана	oorukana
cure	дарылоо	dарıloo
to vaccinate (vt)	эмдөө	emdøø
to be in a coma	комада болуу	komada boluu
intensive care	реанимация	reanimatsija
symptom	белги	belgi
pulse (heartbeat)	тамыр кагышы	tamır kagıʃı

6. Feelings. Emotions. Conversation

I, me	мен, мага	men, maga
you	сен	sen
he, she, it	ал	al

we	биз	biz
you (to a group)	силер	siler
you (polite, sing.)	сиз	siz
you (polite, pl)	сиздер	sizder
they	алар	alar

Hello! (fam.)	Салам!	salam!
Hello! (form.)	Саламатсызбы!	salamatsızbı!
Good morning!	Кутман таңыңыз менен!	kutman taŋıŋız menen!
Good afternoon!	Кутман күнүңүз менен!	kutman kynyŋyz menen!
Good evening!	Кутман кечиңиз менен!	kutman ketʃiŋiz menen!

to say hello	учурашуу	utʃuraʃuu
to greet (vt)	саламдашуу	salamdaʃuu
How are you?	Иштериң кандай?	iʃteriŋ kandaj?
How are you? (form.)	Иштериңиз кандай?	iʃteriŋiz kandaj?
How are you? (fam.)	Иштер кандай?	iʃter kandaj?
Bye-Bye! Goodbye!	Көрүшкөнчө!	køryʃkøntʃø!
Thank you!	Рахмат!	raχmat!

feelings	сезим	sezim
to be hungry	ачка болуу	atʃka boluu
to be thirsty	суусап калуу	suusap kaluu

tired (adj)	чарчаңкы	tʃartʃaŋkı
to be worried	сарсанаа болуу	sarsanaa boluu
to be nervous	тынчы кетүү	tıntʃı ketyy
hope	үмүт	ymyt
to hope (vi, vt)	үмүттөнүү	ymyttønyy

character	мүнөз	mynøz
modest (adj)	жөнөкөй	dʒønøkøj
lazy (adj)	жалкоо	dʒalkoo
generous (adj)	берешен	bereʃen
talented (adj)	зээндүү	zeendyy

honest (adj)	чынчыл	tʃıntʃıl
serious (adj)	оор басырыктуу	oor basırıktuu
shy, timid (adj)	тартынчаак	tartıntʃaak
sincere (adj)	ак ниеттен	ak nietten
coward	суу жүрөк	suu dʒyrøk

to sleep (vi)	уктоо	uktoo
dream	түш	tyʃ
bed	керебет	kerebet
pillow	жаздык	dʒazdık

insomnia	уйкусуздук	ujkusuzduk
to go to bed	уктоого кетүү	uktoogo ketyy
nightmare	коркунучтуу түш	korkunutʃtuu tyʃ
alarm clock	ойготкуч саат	ojgotkutʃ saat

smile	жылмайыш	dʒılmajıʃ
to smile (vi)	жылмаюу	dʒılmadʒuu
to laugh (vi)	күлүү	kylyy

quarrel	уруш	uruʃ
insult	кордоо	kordoo
resentment	таарыныч	taarınıtʃ
angry (mad)	ачууланган	atʃuulangan

7. Clothing. Personal accessories

clothes	кийим	kijim
coat (overcoat)	пальто	palʲto
fur coat	тон	ton
jacket (e.g., leather ~)	күрмө	kyrmø
raincoat (trenchcoat, etc.)	плащ	plaʃtʃ

shirt (button shirt)	көйнөк	køjnøk
pants	шым	ʃım
suit jacket	бешмант	beʃmant
suit	костюм	kostʉm
dress (frock)	көйнөк	køjnøk

skirt	юбка	jʉbka
T-shirt	футболка	futbolka
bathrobe	халат	χalat
pajamas	пижама	piʤama
workwear	жумуш кийим	ʤumuʃ kijim
underwear	ич кийим	iʧ kijim
socks	байпак	bajpak
bra	бюстгальтер	bʉstgalʲter
pantyhose	колготки	kolgotki
stockings (thigh highs)	байпак	bajpak
bathing suit	купальник	kupalʲnik
hat	топу	topu
footwear	бут кийим	but kijim
boots (e.g., cowboy ~)	өтүк	øtyk
heel	така	taka
shoestring	боо	boo
shoe polish	өтүк май	øtyk maj
cotton (n)	пахта	paχta
wool (n)	жүн	ʤyn
fur (n)	тери	teri
gloves	колкап	kolkap
mittens	мээлей	meelej
scarf (muffler)	моюн орогуч	mojʉn oroguʧ
glasses (eyeglasses)	көз айнек	køz ajnek
umbrella	чатырча	ʧatɯrʧa
tie (necktie)	галстук	galstuk
handkerchief	бетаарчы	betaarʧɯ
comb	тарак	tarak
hairbrush	тарак	tarak
buckle	таралга	taralga
belt	кайыш кур	kajɯʃ kur
purse	кичине колбаштык	kiʧine kolbaʃtɯk
collar	жака	ʤaka
pocket	чөнтөк	ʧøntøk
sleeve	жең	ʤeŋ
fly (on trousers)	ширинка	ʃirinka
zipper (fastener)	молния	molnija
button	топчу	topʧu
to get dirty (vi)	булгап алуу	bulgap aluu
stain (mark, spot)	так	tak

8. City. Urban institutions

store	дүкөн	dykøn
shopping mall	соода борбору	sooda borboru
supermarket	супермаркет	supermarket
shoe store	бут кийим дүкөнү	but kijim dykøny
bookstore	китеп дүкөнү	kitep dykøny

drugstore, pharmacy	дарыкана	darıkana
bakery	нан дүкөнү	nan dykøny
pastry shop	кондитердик дүкөн	konditerdik dykøn
grocery store	азык-түлүк	azık-tylyk
butcher shop	эт дүкөнү	et dykøny
produce store	жашылча дүкөнү	dʒaʃiltʃa dykøny
market	базар	bazar

hair salon	чач тарач	tʃatʃ taratʃ
post office	почта	potʃta
dry cleaners	химиялык тазалоо	χimijalık tazaloo
circus	цирк	tsırk
zoo	зоопарк	zoopark

theater	театр	teatr
movie theater	кинотеатр	kinoteatr
museum	музей	muzej
library	китепкана	kitepkana

mosque	мечит	metʃit
synagogue	синагога	sinagoga
cathedral	чоң чиркөө	tʃoŋ tʃirkøø
temple	ибадаткана	ibadatkana
church	чиркөө	tʃirkøø

college	коллеж	kolledʒ
university	университет	universitet
school	мектеп	mektep

hotel	мейманкана	mejmankana
bank	банк	bank
embassy	элчилик	eltʃilik
travel agency	турагенттиги	turagenttigi

subway	метро	metro
hospital	оорукана	oorukana
gas station	май куюучу станция	maj kujuutʃu stantsija
parking lot	унаа токтоочу жай	unaa toktootʃu dʒaj

ENTRANCE	КИРҮҮ	kiryy
EXIT	ЧЫГУУ	tʃiguu
PUSH	ӨЗҮҢҮЗДӨН ТҮРТҮҢҮЗ	øzyŋyzdøn tyrtyŋyz
PULL	ӨЗҮҢҮЗГӨ ТАРТЫҢЫЗ	øzyŋyzgø tartıŋız

| OPEN | АЧЫК | atʃık |
| CLOSED | ЖАБЫК | dʒabık |

monument	эстелик	estelik
fortress	чеп	tʃep
palace	сарай	saraj

medieval (adj)	орто кылымдык	orto kılımdık
ancient (adj)	байыркы	bajırkı
national (adj)	улуттук	uluttuk
famous (monument, etc.)	таанымал	taanımal

9. Money. Finances

money	акча	aktʃa
coin	тыйын	tıjın
dollar	доллар	dollar
euro	евро	evro

ATM	банкомат	bankomat
currency exchange	алмаштыруу пункту	almaʃtıruu punktu
exchange rate	курс	kurs
cash	накталай акча	naktalaj aktʃa

How much?	Канча?	kantʃa?
to pay (vi, vt)	төлөө	tøløø
payment	акы төлөө	akı tøløø
change (give the ~)	кайтарылган майда акча	kajtarılgan majda aktʃa

price	баа	baa
discount	арзандатуу	arzandatuu
cheap (adj)	арзан	arzan
expensive (adj)	кымбат	kımbat

bank	банк	bank
account	эсеп	esep
credit card	насыя картасы	nasıja kartası
check	чек	tʃek
to write a check	чек жазып берүү	tʃek dʒazıp beryy
checkbook	чек китепчеси	tʃek kiteptʃesi

debt	карыз	karız
debtor	карыздар	karızdar
to lend (money)	карызга берүү	karızga beryy
to borrow (vi, vt)	карызга алуу	karızga aluu

to rent (~ a tuxedo)	ижарага алуу	idʒaraga aluu
on credit (adv)	насыяга алуу	nasıjaga aluu
wallet	намыян	namıjan

safe	сейф	sejf
inheritance	мурас	muras
fortune (wealth)	мүлк	mylk

tax	салык	salık
fine	айып	ajıp
to fine (vt)	айып пул салуу	ajıp pul saluu

wholesale (adj)	дүңүнөн	dyŋynøn
retail (adj)	чекене	tʃekene
to insure (vt)	камсыздандыруу	kamsızdandıruu
insurance	камсыздандыруу	kamsızdandıruu

capital	капитал	kapital
turnover	жүгүртүлүш	dʒygyrtylyʃ
stock (share)	акция	aktsija
profit	пайда	pajda
profitable (adj)	майнаптуу	majnaptuu

crisis	каатчылык	kaattʃılık
bankruptcy	кудуретсиздик	kuduretsizdik
to go bankrupt	кудуретсиз калуу	kuduretsiz kaluu

accountant	бухгалтер	buχgalter
salary	кызмат акы	kızmat akı
bonus (money)	сыйлык	sıjlık

10. Transportation

bus	автобус	avtobus
streetcar	трамвай	tramvaj
trolley bus	троллейбус	trollejbus

to go by ...	... жүрүү	... dʒyryy
to get on (~ the bus)	... отуруу	... oturuu
to get off ...	... түшүп калуу	... tyʃyp kaluu

stop (e.g., bus ~)	аялдама	ajaldama
terminus	акыркы аялдама	akırkı ajaldama
schedule	ырааттама	ıraattama
ticket	билет	bilet
to be late (for ...)	кечигүү	ketʃigyy

taxi, cab	такси	taksi
by taxi	таксиде	takside
taxi stand	такси токтоочу жай	taksi toktootʃu dʒaj

traffic	көчө кыймылы	køtʃø kıjmılı
rush hour	кызуу маал	kızuu maal
to park (vi)	токтотуу	toktotuu

subway	метро	metro
station	бекет	beket
train	поезд	poezd
train station	вокзал	vokzal
rails	рельсалар	relʲsalar
compartment	купе	kupe
berth	текче	tektʃe

airplane	учак	utʃak
air ticket	авиабилет	aviabilet
airline	авиакомпания	aviakompanija
airport	аэропорт	aeroport

flight (act of flying)	учуу	utʃuu
luggage	жүк	dʒyk
luggage cart	араба	araba

ship	кеме	keme
cruise ship	лайнер	lajner
yacht	яхта	jaχta
boat (flat-bottomed ~)	кайык	kajık

captain	капитан	kapitan
cabin	каюта	kajᵿta
port (harbor)	порт	port

bicycle	велосипед	velosiped
scooter	мотороллер	motoroller
motorcycle, bike	мотоцикл	mototsikl
pedal	педаль	pedalʲ
pump	соркыскыч	sorkıskıtʃ
wheel	дөңгөлөк	døŋgøløk

automobile, car	автоунаа	avtounaa
ambulance	тез жардам	tez dʒardam
truck	жүк ташуучу машина	dʒyk taʃuutʃu maʃina
used (adj)	колдонулган	koldonulgan
car crash	авто урунушу	avto urunuʃu
repair	оңдоо	oŋdoo

11. Food. Part 1

meat	эт	et
chicken	тоок	took
duck	өрдөк	ørdøk

pork	чочко эти	tʃotʃko eti
veal	торпок эти	torpok eti
lamb	кой эти	koj eti
beef	уй эти	uj eti

sausage (bologna, etc.)	колбаса	kolbasa
egg	жумуртка	dʒumurtka
fish	балык	balık
cheese	сыр	sır
sugar	кум шекер	kum-ʃeker
salt	туз	tuz
rice	күрүч	kyrytʃ
pasta (macaroni)	макарон	makaron
butter	ак май	ak maj
vegetable oil	өсүмдүк майы	øsymdyk majı
bread	нан	nan
chocolate (n)	шоколад	ʃokolad
wine	шарап	ʃarap
coffee	кофе	kofe
milk	сүт	syt
juice	шире	ʃire
beer	сыра	sıra
tea	чай	tʃaj
tomato	помидор	pomidor
cucumber	бадыраң	badıraŋ
carrot	сабиз	sabiz
potato	картошка	kartoʃka
onion	пияз	pijaz
garlic	сарымсак	sarımsak
cabbage	капуста	kapusta
beet	кызылча	kızıltʃa
eggplant	баклажан	bakladʒan
dill	укроп	ukrop
lettuce	салат	salat
corn (maize)	жүгөрү	dʒygøry
fruit	мөмө	mømø
apple	алма	alma
pear	алмурут	almurut
lemon	лимон	limon
orange	апельсин	apelʲsin
strawberry (garden ~)	кулпунай	kulpunaj
plum	кара өрүк	kara øryk
raspberry	дан куурай	dan kuuraj
pineapple	ананас	ananas
banana	банан	banan
watermelon	арбуз	arbuz
grape	жүзүм	dʒyzym
melon	коон	koon

12. Food. Part 2

cuisine	даам	daam
recipe	тамак жасоо ыкмасы	tamak dʒasoo ıkması
food	тамак	tamak
to have breakfast	эртең менен тамактануу	erteŋ menen tamaktanuu
to have lunch	түштөнүү	tyʃtønyy
to have dinner	кечки тамакты ичүү	ketʃki tamaktı itʃyy
taste, flavor	даам	daam
tasty (adj)	даамдуу	daamduu
cold (adj)	муздак	muzdak
hot (adj)	ысык	ısık
sweet (sugary)	таттуу	tattuu
salty (adj)	туздуу	tuzduu
sandwich (bread)	бутерброд	buterbrod
side dish	гарнир	garnir
filling (for cake, pie)	начинка	natʃinka
sauce	соус	sous
piece (of cake, pie)	бөлүк	bølyk
diet	мүнөз тамак	mynøz tamak
vitamin	витамин	vitamin
calorie	калория	kalorija
vegetarian (n)	эттен чанган	etten tʃangan
restaurant	ресторан	restoran
coffee house	кофекана	kofekana
appetite	табит	tabit
Enjoy your meal!	Тамагыңыз таттуу болсун!	tamagıŋız tattuu bolsun!
waiter	официант	ofitsiant
waitress	официант кыз	ofitsiant kız
bartender	бармен	barmen
menu	меню	menu
spoon	кашык	kaʃık
knife	бычак	bıtʃak
fork	вилка	vilka
cup (e.g., coffee ~)	чөйчөк	tʃøjtʃøk
plate (dinner ~)	табак	tabak
saucer	табак	tabak
napkin (on table)	майлык	majlık
toothpick	тиш чукугуч	tiʃ tʃukugutʃ
to order (meal)	буйрутма кылуу	bujrutma kıluu
course, dish	тамак	tamak

portion	порция	portsija
appetizer	ысылык	ısılık
salad	салат	salat
soup	сорпо	sorpo

dessert	десерт	desert
jam (whole fruit jam)	кыям	kıjam
ice-cream	бал муздак	bal muzdak

check	эсеп	esep
to pay the check	эсеп төлөө	esep tøløø
tip	чайпул	tʃajpul

13. House. Apartment. Part 1

house	үй	yj
country house	шаар четиндеги үй	ʃaar tʃetindegi yj
villa (seaside ~)	вилла	villa

floor, story	кабат	kabat
entrance	подъезд	podʰjezd
wall	дубал	dubal
roof	чатыр	tʃatır
chimney	мор	mor

attic (storage place)	чердак	tʃerdak
window	терезе	tereze
window ledge	текче	tektʃe
balcony	балкон	balkon

stairs (stairway)	тепкич	tepkitʃ
mailbox	почта ящиги	potʃta jaʃtʃigi
garbage can	таштанды челеги	taʃtandı tʃelegi
elevator	лифт	lift

electricity	электр кубаты	elektr kubatı
light bulb	чырак	tʃırak
switch	өчүргүч	øtʃyrgytʃ
wall socket	розетка	rozetka
fuse	эриме сактагыч	erime saktagıtʃ

door	эшик	eʃik
handle, doorknob	тутка	tutka
key	ачкыч	atʃkıtʃ
doormat	килемче	kilemtʃe

door lock	кулпу	kulpu
doorbell	коңгуроо	konguroo
knock (at the door)	такылдатуу	takıldatuu
to knock (vi)	такылдатуу	takıldatuu

peephole	көзчө	køztʃø
yard	эшик	eʃik
garden	бакча	baktʃa
swimming pool	бассейн	bassejn
gym (home gym)	машыгуу залы	maʃɪguu zalɪ
tennis court	теннис корту	tennis kortu
garage	гараж	garadʒ

private property	жеке менчик	dʒeke mentʃik
warning sign	эскертүү белгиси	eskertyy belgisi
security	күзөт	kyzøt
security guard	кароолчу	karooltʃu

renovations	ремонт	remont
to renovate (vt)	ремонт жасоо	remont dʒasoo
to put in order	иретке келтирүү	iretke keltiryy
to paint (~ a wall)	боео	boeo
wallpaper	туш кагаз	tuʃ kagaz
to varnish (vt)	лак менен жабуу	lak menen dʒabuu

pipe	түтүк	tytyk
tools	аспаптар	aspaptar
basement	жер асты	dʒer astɪ
sewerage (system)	канализация	kanalizatsija

14. House. Apartment. Part 2

apartment	батир	batir
room	бөлмө	bølmø
bedroom	уктоочу бөлмө	uktootʃu bølmø
dining room	ашкана	aʃkana

living room	конок үйү	konok yjy
study (home office)	иш бөлмөсү	iʃ bølmøsy
entry room	кире бериш	kire beriʃ
bathroom (room with a bath or shower)	ванная	vannaja
half bath	дааратхана	daaratkana

floor	пол	pol
ceiling	шып	ʃɪp

to dust (vt)	чаң сүртүү	tʃaŋ syrtyy
vacuum cleaner	чаң соргуч	tʃaŋ sorgutʃ
to vacuum (vt)	чаң сордуруу	tʃaŋ sorduruu

mop	швабра	ʃvabra
dust cloth	чүпүрөк	tʃypyrøk
short broom	шыпыргы	ʃɪpɪrgɪ
dustpan	калак	kalak

furniture	эмерек	emerek
table	стол	stol
chair	стул	stul
armchair	олпок отургуч	olpok oturgutʃ
bookcase	китеп шкафы	kitep ʃkafı
shelf	текче	tektʃe
wardrobe	шкаф	ʃkaf
mirror	күзгү	kyzgy
carpet	килем	kilem
fireplace	очок	otʃok
drapes	парда	parda
table lamp	стол чырагы	stol tʃıragı
chandelier	асма шам	asma ʃam
kitchen	ашкана	aʃkana
gas stove (range)	газ плитасы	gaz plitası
electric stove	электр плитасы	elektr plitası
microwave oven	микротолкун меши	mikrotolkun meʃi
refrigerator	муздаткыч	muzdatkıtʃ
freezer	тоңдургуч	toŋdurgutʃ
dishwasher	идиш жуучу машина	idiʃ dʒuutʃu maʃina
faucet	чорго	tʃorgo
meat grinder	эт туурагыч	et tuuragıtʃ
juicer	шире сыккыч	ʃire sıkkıtʃ
toaster	тостер	toster
mixer	миксер	mikser
coffee machine	кофе кайнаткыч	kofe kajnatkıtʃ
kettle	чайнек	tʃajnek
teapot	чайнек	tʃajnek
TV set	сыналгы	sınalgı
VCR (video recorder)	видеомагнитофон	videomagnitofon
iron (e.g., steam ~)	үтүк	ytyk
telephone	телефон	telefon

15. Professions. Social status

director	директор	direktor
superior	башчы	baʃtʃı
president	президент	prezident
assistant	жардамчы	dʒardamtʃı
secretary	катчы	kattʃı
owner, proprietor	ээси	eesi
partner	өнөктөш	ønøktøʃ

stockholder	акция кармоочу	aktsija karmootʃu
businessman	бизнесмен	biznesmen
millionaire	миллионер	millioner
billionaire	миллиардер	milliarder

actor	актёр	aktʲor
architect	архитектор	arχitektor
banker	банкир	bankir
broker	далдалчы	daldaltʃı

veterinarian	мал доктуру	mal dokturu
doctor	доктур	doktur
chambermaid	үй кызматкери	yj kızmatkeri
designer	дизайнер	dizajner
correspondent	кабарчы	kabartʃı
delivery man	жеткирүүчү	dʒetkiryytʃy

electrician	электрик	elektrik
musician	музыкант	muzıkant
babysitter	бала баккыч	bala bakkıtʃ
hairdresser	чач тарач	tʃatʃ taratʃ
herder, shepherd	чабан	tʃaban

singer (masc.)	ырчы	ırtʃı
translator	котормочу	kotormotʃu
writer	жазуучу	dʒazuutʃu
carpenter	жыгач уста	dʒıgatʃ usta
cook	ашпозчу	aʃpoztʃu

fireman	өрт өчүргүч	ørt øtʃyrgytʃ
police officer	полиция кызматкери	politsija kızmatkeri
mailman	кат ташуучу	kat taʃuutʃu
programmer	программист	programmist
salesman (store staff)	сатуучу	satuutʃu

worker	жумушчу	dʒumuʃtʃu
gardener	багбанчы	bagbantʃı
plumber	сантехник	santeχnik
dentist	тиш доктур	tiʃ doktur
flight attendant (fem.)	стюардесса	stuardessa

| dancer (masc.) | бийчи жигит | bijtʃi dʒigit |
| bodyguard | жан сакчы | dʒan saktʃı |

| scientist | илимпоз | ilimpoz |
| schoolteacher | мугалим | mugalim |

farmer	фермер	fermer
surgeon	хирург	χirurg
miner	кенчи	kentʃi
chef (kitchen chef)	башкы ашпозчу	baʃkı aʃpoztʃu
driver	айдоочу	ajdootʃu

16. Sport

kind of sports	спорттун түрү	sporttun tyry
soccer	футбол	futbol
hockey	хоккей	χokkej
basketball	баскетбол	basketbol
baseball	бейсбол	bejsbol
volleyball	волейбол	volejbol
boxing	бокс	boks
wrestling	күрөш	kyrøʃ
tennis	теннис	tennis
swimming	сүзүү	syzyy
chess	шахмат	ʃaχmat
running	чуркоо	ʧurkoo
athletics	жеңил атлетика	dʒeŋil atletika
figure skating	муз бийи	muz biji
cycling	велоспорт	velosport
billiards	бильярд	biljard
bodybuilding	бодибилдинг	bodibilding
golf	гольф	golʲf
scuba diving	сууга чөмүүчү	suuga ʧømyyʧy
sailing	парус астында сызуу	parus astında sızuu
archery	жаа атуу	dʒaa atuu
period, half	тайм	tajm
half-time	тыныгуу	tınıguu
tie	теңме-тең	teŋme-teŋ
to tie (vi)	теңме-тең бүтүрүү	teŋme-teŋ bytyryy
treadmill	тегеретме	tegeretme
player	оюнчу	ojʉnʧu
substitute	кезектеги оюнчу	kezektegi ojʉnʧu
substitutes bench	кезек отургучу	kezek oturgutʃu
match	матч	matʧ
goal	дарбаза	darbaza
goalkeeper	дарбазачы	darbazatʃı
goal (score)	гол	gol
Olympic Games	Олимпиада Оюндары	olimpiada ojʉndarı
to set a record	рекорд коюу	rekord kojʉu
final	финал	final
champion	чемпион	ʧempion
championship	чемпионат	ʧempionat
winner	жеңүүчү	dʒeŋyyʧy
victory	жеңиш	dʒeŋiʃ
to win (vi)	утуу	utuu

| to lose (not win) | жеңилүү | dʒeŋilyy |
| medal | медаль | medalʲ |

first place	биринчи орун	birintʃi orun
second place	экинчи орун	ekintʃi orun
third place	үчүнчү орун	ytʃyntʃy orun

stadium	стадион	stadion
fan, supporter	күйөрман	kyjørman
trainer, coach	машыктыруучу	maʃiktiruutʃu
training	машыгуу	maʃiguu

17. Foreign languages. Orthography

language	тил	til
to study (vt)	окуу	okuu
pronunciation	айтылышы	ajtiliʃi
accent	акцент	aktsent

noun	зат атооч	zat atootʃ
adjective	сын атооч	sin atootʃ
verb	этиш	etiʃ
adverb	тактооч	taktootʃ

pronoun	ат атооч	at atootʃ
interjection	сырдык сөз	sirdik søz
preposition	препозиция	prepozitsija

root	сөздүн уңгусу	søzdyn uŋgusu
ending	жалгоо	dʒalgoo
prefix	префикс	prefiks
syllable	муун	muun
suffix	суффикс	suffiks

stress mark	басым	basim
period, dot	чекит	tʃekit
comma	үтүр	ytyr
colon	кош чекит	koʃ tʃekit
ellipsis	көп чекит	køp tʃekit

question	суроо	suroo
question mark	суроо белгиси	suroo belgisi
exclamation point	илеп белгиси	ilep belgisi

in quotation marks	тырмакчага алынган	tirmaktʃaga alingan
in parenthesis	кашаага алынган	kaʃaaga alingan
letter	тамга	tamga
capital letter	баш тамга	baʃ tamga
sentence	сүйлөм	syjløm
group of words	сөз айкашы	søz ajkaʃi

expression	туюнтма	tujuntma
subject	сүйлөмдүн ээси	syjlømdyn eesi
predicate	баяндооч	bajandootʃ
line	сап	sap
paragraph	абзац	abzaʦ
synonym	синоним	sinonim
antonym	антоним	antonim
exception	чектен чыгаруу	tʃekten tʃɪgaruu
to underline (vt)	баса белгилөө	basa belgiløø
rules	эрежелер	eredʒeler
grammar	грамматика	grammatika
vocabulary	лексика	leksika
phonetics	фонетика	fonetika
alphabet	алфавит	alfavit
textbook	китеп	kitep
dictionary	сөздүк	søzdyk
phrasebook	тилачар	tilatʃar
word	сөз	søz
meaning	маани	maani
memory	эс тутум	es tutum

18. The Earth. Geography

the Earth	Жер	dʒer
the globe (the Earth)	жер шары	dʒer ʃarɪ
planet	планета	planeta
geography	география	geografija
nature	табийгат	tabijgat
map	карта	karta
atlas	атлас	atlas
in the north	түндүктө	tyndyktø
in the south	түштүктө	tyʃtyktø
in the west	батышта	batɪʃta
in the east	чыгышта	tʃɪgɪʃta
sea	деңиз	deŋiz
ocean	мухит	muχit
gulf (bay)	булуң	buluŋ
straits	кысык	kɪsɪk
continent (mainland)	материк	materik
island	арал	aral
peninsula	жарым арал	dʒarɪm aral
archipelago	архипелаг	arχipelag

harbor	гавань	gavanʲ
coral reef	маржан рифи	mardʒan rifi
shore	жээк	dʒeek
coast	жээк	dʒeek

| flow (flood tide) | суунун көтөрүлүшү | suunun køtørylyʃy |
| ebb (ebb tide) | суунун тартылуусу | suunun tartıluusu |

latitude	кеңдик	keŋdik
longitude	узундук	uzunduk
parallel	параллель	parallelʲ
equator	экватор	ekvator

sky	асман	asman
horizon	горизонт	gorizont
atmosphere	атмосфера	atmosfera

mountain	тоо	too
summit, top	чоку	tʃoku
cliff	зоока	zooka
hill	дөбө	døbø

volcano	вулкан	vulkan
glacier	муз	muz
waterfall	шаркыратма	ʃarkıratma
plain	түздүк	tyzdyk

river	дарыя	darıja
spring (natural source)	булак	bulak
bank (of river)	жээк	dʒeek
downstream (adv)	агым боюнча	agım bojɵntʃa
upstream (adv)	агымга каршы	agımga karʃı

lake	көл	køl
dam	тогоон	togoon
canal	канал	kanal
swamp (marshland)	саз	saz
ice	муз	muz

19. Countries of the world. Part 1

Europe	Европа	evropa
European Union	Европа Биримдиги	evropa birimdigi
European (n)	европалык	evropalık
European (adj)	европалык	evropalık

Austria	Австрия	avstrija
Great Britain	Улуу Британия	uluu britanija
England	Англия	anglija
Belgium	Бельгия	belʲgija

Germany	**Германия**	germanija
Netherlands	**Нидерланддар**	niderlanddar
Holland	**Голландия**	gollandija
Greece	**Греция**	greʦija
Denmark	**Дания**	danija
Ireland	**Ирландия**	irlandija
Iceland	**Исландия**	islandija
Spain	**Испания**	ispanija
Italy	**Италия**	italija
Cyprus	**Кипр**	kipr
Malta	**Мальта**	malʲta
Norway	**Норвегия**	norvegija
Portugal	**Португалия**	portugalija
Finland	**Финляндия**	finlʲandija
France	**Франция**	franʦija
Sweden	**Швеция**	ʃveʦija
Switzerland	**Швейцария**	ʃvejʦarija
Scotland	**Шотландия**	ʃotlandija
Vatican	**Ватикан**	vatikan
Liechtenstein	**Лихтенштейн**	liχtenʃtejn
Luxembourg	**Люксембург**	lʉksemburg
Monaco	**Монако**	monako
Albania	**Албания**	albanija
Bulgaria	**Болгария**	bolgarija
Hungary	**Венгрия**	vengrija
Latvia	**Латвия**	latvija
Lithuania	**Литва**	litva
Poland	**Польша**	polʲʃa
Romania	**Румыния**	rumınija
Serbia	**Сербия**	serbija
Slovakia	**Словакия**	slovakija
Croatia	**Хорватия**	χorvatija
Czech Republic	**Чехия**	ʧeχija
Estonia	**Эстония**	estonija
Bosnia and Herzegovina	**Босния жана**	bosnija ʤana
Macedonia (Republic of ~)	**Македония**	makedonija
Slovenia	**Словения**	slovenija
Montenegro	**Черногория**	ʧernogorija
Belarus	**Беларусь**	belarusʲ
Moldova, Moldavia	**Молдова**	moldova
Russia	**Россия**	rossija
Ukraine	**Украина**	ukraina

20. Countries of the world. Part 2

Asia	Азия	azija
Vietnam	Вьетнам	vjetnam
India	Индия	indija
Israel	Израиль	izrailʲ
China	Кытай	kıtaj

Lebanon	Ливан	livan
Mongolia	Монголия	mongolija
Malaysia	Малазия	malazija
Pakistan	Пакистан	pakistan
Saudi Arabia	Сауд Аравиясы	saud aravijası

Thailand	Таиланд	tailand
Taiwan	Тайвань	tajvanʲ
Turkey	Түркия	tyrkija
Japan	Япония	japonija
Afghanistan	Оогланстан	ooganstan

Bangladesh	Бангладеш	bangladeʃ
Indonesia	Индонезия	indonezija
Jordan	Иордания	iordanija
Iraq	Ирак	irak
Iran	Иран	iran

Cambodia	Камбожа	kambodʒa
Kuwait	Кувейт	kuvejt
Laos	Лаос	laos
Myanmar	Мьянма	mjanma
Nepal	Непал	nepal

United Arab Emirates	Бириккен Араб Эмираттары	birikken arab emirattarı
Syria	Сирия	sirija
Palestine	Палестина	palestina
South Korea	Түштүк Корея	tyʃtyk koreja
North Korea	Түндүк Корея	tundyk koreja

United States of America	Америка Кошмо Штаттары	amerika koʃmo ʃtattarı
Canada	Канада	kanada
Mexico	Мексика	meksika
Argentina	Аргентина	argentina
Brazil	Бразилия	brazilija

Colombia	Колумбия	kolumbija
Cuba	Куба	kuba
Chile	Чили	tʃili
Venezuela	Венесуэла	venesuela
Ecuador	Эквадор	ekvador

The Bahamas	Багам аралдары	bagam araldarı
Panama	Панама	panama
Egypt	Египет	egipet
Morocco	Марокко	marokko
Tunisia	Тунис	tunis
Kenya	Кения	kenija
Libya	Ливия	livija
South Africa	ТАР	tar
Australia	Австралия	avstralija
New Zealand	Жаңы Зеландия	dʒaɲı zelandija

21. Weather. Natural disasters

weather	аба-ырайы	aba-ırajı
weather forecast	аба-ырайы боюнча маалымат	aba-ırajı bojʉntʃa maalımat
temperature	температура	temperatura
thermometer	термометр	termometr
barometer	барометр	barometr
sun	күн	kyn
to shine (vi)	күн тийүү	kyn tijyy
sunny (day)	күн ачык	kyn atʃık
to come up (vi)	чыгуу	tʃıguu
to set (vi)	батуу	batuu
rain	жамгыр	dʒamgır
it's raining	жамгыр жаап жатат	dʒamgır dʒaap dʒatat
pouring rain	нөшөрлөгөн жаан	nøʃørløgøn dʒaan
rain cloud	булут	bulut
puddle	көлчүк	køltʃyk
to get wet (in rain)	суу болуу	suu boluu
thunderstorm	чагылгандуу жаан	tʃagılganduu dʒaan
lightning (~ strike)	чагылган	tʃagılgan
to flash (vi)	жарк этүү	dʒark etyy
thunder	күн күркүрөө	kyn kyrkyrøø
it's thundering	күн күркүрөп жатат	kyn kyrkyrøp dʒatat
hail	мөндүр	møndyr
it's hailing	мөндүр түшүп жатат	møndyr tyʃyp dʒatat
heat (extreme ~)	ысык	ısık
it's hot	ысык	ısık
it's warm	жылуу	dʒıluu
it's cold	суук	suuk
fog (mist)	туман	tuman
foggy	тумандуу	tumanduu
cloud	булут	bulut

| cloudy (adj) | булуттуу | buluttuu |
| humidity | ным | nım |

snow	кар	kar
it's snowing	кар жаап жатат	kar dʒaap dʒatat
frost (severe ~, freezing cold)	аяз	ajaz
below zero (adv)	нольдон төмөн	nolʲdon tөmөn
hoarfrost	кыроо	kıroo

bad weather	жаан-чачындуу күн	dʒaan-tʃatʃınduu kyn
disaster	кыйроо	kıjroo
flood, inundation	ташкын	taʃkın
avalanche	көчкү	kөtʃky
earthquake	жер титирөө	dʒer titirөө

tremor, shoke	жердин силкиниши	dʒerdin silkiniʃi
epicenter	эпицентр	epitsentr
eruption	атырылып чыгуу	atırılıp tʃıguu
lava	лава	lava

tornado	торнадо	tornado
twister	куюн	kujʉn
hurricane	бороон	boroon
tsunami	цунами	tsunami
cyclone	циклон	tsıklon

22. Animals. Part 1

| animal | жаныбар | dʒanıbar |
| predator | жырткыч | dʒırtkıtʃ |

tiger	жолборс	dʒolbors
lion	арстан	arstan
wolf	карышкыр	karıʃkır
fox	түлкү	tylky
jaguar	ягуар	jaguar

lynx	сүлөөсүн	sylөөsyn
coyote	койот	kojot
jackal	чөө	tʃөө
hyena	гиена	giena

squirrel	тыйын чычкан	tıjın tʃıtʃkan
hedgehog	кирпичечен	kirpitʃetʃen
rabbit	коен	koen
raccoon	енот	enot

| hamster | хомяк | χomʲak |
| mole | момолой | momoloj |

mouse	чычкан	t͡ʃɯt͡ʃkan
rat	келемиш	kelemiʃ
bat	жарганат	d͡ʒarganat

beaver	кемчет	kemt͡ʃet
horse	жылкы	d͡ʒɯlkɯ
deer	бугу	bugu
camel	төө	tøø
zebra	зебра	zebra

whale	кит	kit
seal	тюлень	tʉlenʲ
walrus	морж	mord͡ʒ
dolphin	дельфин	delʲfin

bear	аюу	ajʉu
monkey	маймыл	majmɯl
elephant	пил	pil
rhinoceros	керик	kerik
giraffe	жираф	d͡ʒiraf

hippopotamus	бегемот	begemot
kangaroo	кенгуру	kenguru
cat	ургаачы мышык	urgaat͡ʃɯ mɯʃɯk
dog	ит	it

cow	уй	uj
bull	бука	buka
sheep (ewe)	кой	koj
goat	эчки	et͡ʃki

donkey	эшек	eʃek
pig, hog	чочко	t͡ʃot͡ʃko
hen (chicken)	тоок	took
rooster	короз	koroz

duck	өрдөк	ørdøk
goose	каз	kaz
turkey (hen)	ургаачы күрп	urgaat͡ʃɯ kyrp
sheepdog	овчарка	ovt͡ʃarka

23. Animals. Part 2

bird	куш	kuʃ
pigeon	көгүчкөн	køgyt͡ʃkøn
sparrow	таранчы	tarant͡ʃɯ
tit (great tit)	синица	sinit͡sa
magpie	сагызган	sagɯzgan
eagle	бүркүт	byrkyt
hawk	ителги	itelgi

falcon	шумкар	ʃumkar
swan	аккуу	akkuu
crane	турна	turna
stork	илегилек	ilegilek
parrot	тотукуш	totukuʃ
peacock	тоос	toos
ostrich	төө куш	tøø kuʃ

heron	көк кытан	køk kıtan
nightingale	булбул	bulbul
swallow	чабалекей	tʃabalekej
woodpecker	тоңкулдак	toŋkuldak
cuckoo	күкүк	kykyk
owl	мыкый үкү	mıkıj yky

penguin	пингвин	pingvin
tuna	тунец	tuneʦ
trout	форель	forelʲ
eel	угорь	ugorʲ

shark	акула	akula
crab	краб	krab
jellyfish	медуза	meduza
octopus	сегиз бут	segiz but

starfish	деңиз жылдызы	deŋiz dʒıldızı
sea urchin	деңиз кирписи	deŋiz kirpisi
seahorse	деңиз тайы	deŋiz tajı
shrimp	креветка	krevetka

snake	жылан	dʒılan
viper	кара чаар жылан	kara tʃaar dʒılan
lizard	кескелдирик	keskeldirik
iguana	игуана	iguana

| chameleon | хамелеон | χameleon |
| scorpion | чаян | tʃajan |

turtle	ташбака	taʃbaka
frog	бака	baka
crocodile	крокодил	krokodil

| insect, bug | курт-кумурска | kurt-kumurska |
| butterfly | көпөлөк | køpøløk |

| ant | кумурска | kumurska |
| fly | чымын | tʃımın |

mosquito	чиркей	tʃirkej
beetle	коңуз	koŋuz
bee	бал аары	bal aarı
spider	жөргөмүш	dʒørgømyʃ

24. Trees. Plants

tree	дарак	darak
birch	ак кайың	ak kajıŋ
oak	эмен	emen
linden tree	жөкө дарак	dʒøkø darak
aspen	бай терек	baj terek

maple	клён	klʲon
spruce	кара карагай	kara karagaj
pine	карагай	karagaj
cedar	кедр	kedr

poplar	терек	terek
rowan	четин	tʃetin
beech	бук	buk
elm	кара жыгач	kara dʒıgatʃ

ash (tree)	ясень	jasenʲ
chestnut	каштан	kaʃtan
palm tree	пальма	palʲma
bush	бадал	badal

mushroom	козу карын	kozu karın
poisonous mushroom	уулуу козу карын	uuluu kozu karın
cep (Boletus edulis)	ак козу карын	ak kozu karın
russula	сыроежка	sıroedʒka
fly agaric	мухомор	muχomor
death cap	поганка	poganka

flower	гүл	gyl
bouquet (of flowers)	десте	deste
rose (flower)	роза	roza
tulip	жоогазын	dʒoogazın
carnation	гвоздика	gvozdika

camomile	ромашка	romaʃka
cactus	кактус	kaktus
lily of the valley	ландыш	landıʃ
snowdrop	байчечекей	bajtʃetʃekej
water lily	чөмүч баш	tʃømytʃ baʃ

conservatory (greenhouse)	күнөскана	kynøskana
lawn	газон	gazon
flowerbed	клумба	klumba

plant	өсүмдүк	øsymdyk
grass	чөп	tʃøp
leaf	жалбырак	dʒalbırak
petal	гүлдүн желекчеси	gyldyn dʒelektʃesi
stem	сабак	sabak

young plant (shoot)	өсмө	øsmø
cereal crops	дан эгиндери	dan eginderi
wheat	буудай	buudaj
rye	кара буудай	kara buudaj
oats	сулу	sulu
millet	таруу	taruu
barley	арпа	arpa
corn	жүгөрү	dʒygøry
rice	күрүч	kyrytʃ

25. Various useful words

balance (of situation)	теңдем	teŋdem
base (basis)	түп	typ
beginning	башталыш	baʃtalıʃ
category	категория	kategorija
choice	тандоо	tandoo
coincidence	дал келгендик	dal kelgendik
comparison	салыштырма	salıʃtırma
degree (extent, amount)	даража	daradʒa
development	өнүгүү	ønygyy
difference	айырма	ajırma
effect (e.g., of drugs)	таасир	taasir
effort (exertion)	күч аракет	kytʃ araket
element	элемент	element
example (illustration)	мисал	misal
fact	далил	dalil
help	жардам	dʒardam
ideal	идеал	ideal
kind (sort, type)	түр	tyr
mistake, error	ката	kata
moment	учур	utʃur
obstacle	тоскоолдук	toskoolduk
part (~ of sth)	бөлүгү	bølygy
pause (break)	тыныгуу	tınıguu
position	позиция	pozitsija
problem	көйгөй	køjgøj
process	жараян	dʒarajan
progress	өнүгүү	ønygyy
property (quality)	касиет	kasiet
reaction	реакция	reaktsija
risk	тобокел	tobokel

secret	сыр	sır
series	катар	katar

shape (outer form)	тариз	tariz
situation	кырдаал	kırdaal
solution	чечүү	tʃetʃyy
standard (adj)	стандарттуу	standarttuu

stop (pause)	токтотуу	toktotuu
style	стиль	stilʲ
system	тутум	tutum
table (chart)	жадыбал	dʒadıbal
tempo, rate	темп	temp

term (word, expression)	атоо	atoo
truth (e.g., moment of ~)	чындык	tʃındık
turn (please wait your ~)	кезек	kezek
urgent (adj)	шашылыш	ʃaʃılıʃ

utility (usefulness)	пайда	pajda
variant (alternative)	вариант	variant
way (means, method)	ыкма	ıkma
zone	алкак	alkak

26. Modifiers. Adjectives. Part 1

additional (adj)	кошумча	koʃumtʃa
ancient (~ civilization)	байыркы	bajırkı
artificial (adj)	жасалма	dʒasalma
bad (adj)	жаман	dʒaman
beautiful (person)	сулуу	suluu

big (in size)	чоң	tʃoŋ
bitter (taste)	ачуу	atʃuu
blind (sightless)	сокур	sokur
central (adj)	борбордук	borborduk

children's (adj)	балдар	baldar
clandestine (secret)	жашыруун	dʒaʃıruun
clean (free from dirt)	таза	taza
clever (smart)	акылдуу	akılduu
compatible (adj)	сыйышкыч	sıjıʃkıtʃ

contented (satisfied)	курсант	kursant
dangerous (adj)	коркунучтуу	korkunutʃtuu
dead (not alive)	өлүк	ølyk
dense (fog, smoke)	коюу	kojʉu
difficult (decision)	оор	oor
dirty (not clean)	кир	kir
easy (not difficult)	женил	dʒenil

empty (glass, room)	бош	boʃ
exact (amount)	так	tak
excellent (adj)	мыкты	mıktı

excessive (adj)	ашыкча	aʃıktʃa
exterior (adj)	тышкы	tıʃkı
fast (quick)	тез	tez
fertile (land, soil)	түшүмдүү	tyʃymdyy
fragile (china, glass)	морт	mort

free (at no cost)	акысыз	akısız
fresh (~ water)	тузсуз	tuzsuz
frozen (food)	тоңдурулган	toŋdurulgan
full (completely filled)	толо	tolo
happy (adj)	бактылуу	baktıluu

hard (not soft)	катуу	katuu
huge (adj)	зор	zor
ill (sick, unwell)	оорулуу	ooruluu
immobile (adj)	кыймылсыз	kıjmılsız
important (adj)	маанилүү	maanilyy

interior (adj)	ички	itʃki
last (e.g., ~ week)	мурунку	murunku
last (final)	акыркы	akırkı
left (e.g., ~ side)	сол	sol
legal (legitimate)	мыйзамдуу	mıjzamduu

light (in weight)	жеңил	dʒeŋil
liquid (fluid)	суюк	sujʉk
long (e.g., ~ hair)	узак	uzak
loud (voice, etc.)	катуу	katuu
low (voice)	акырын	akırın

27. Modifiers. Adjectives. Part 2

main (principal)	негизги	negizgi
matt, matte	жалтырабаган	dʒaltırabagan
mysterious (adj)	сырдуу	sırduu
narrow (street, etc.)	кууш	kuuʃ
native (~ country)	өз	øz

negative (~ response)	терс	ters
new (adj)	жаңы	dʒaŋı
next (e.g., ~ week)	кийинки	kijinki
normal (adj)	кадимки	kadimki
not difficult (adj)	анчейин оор эмес	antʃejin oor emes

obligatory (adj)	милдеттүү	mildettyy
old (house)	эски	eski

open (adj)	**ачык**	atʃık
opposite (adj)	**карама-каршы**	karama-karʃı
ordinary (usual)	**жөнөкөй**	dʒønøkøj
original (unusual)	**бөтөнчө**	bøtøntʃø
personal (adj)	**жекелик**	dʒekelik
polite (adj)	**сылык**	sılık
poor (not rich)	**кедей**	kedej
possible (adj)	**мүмкүн**	mymkyn
principal (main)	**негизги**	negizgi
probable (adj)	**ыктымал**	ıktımal
prolonged (e.g., ~ applause)	**узак**	uzak
public (open to all)	**коомдук**	koomduk
rare (adj)	**сейрек**	sejrek
raw (uncooked)	**чийки**	tʃijki
right (not left)	**оң**	oŋ
ripe (fruit)	**бышкан**	bıʃkan
risky (adj)	**тобокелдүү**	tobokeldyy
sad (~ look)	**кайгылуу**	kajgıluu
second hand (adj)	**мурдагы**	murdagı
shallow (water)	**тайыз**	tajız
sharp (blade, etc.)	**курч**	kurtʃ
short (in length)	**кыска**	kıska
similar (adj)	**окшош**	okʃoʃ
small (in size)	**кичине**	kitʃine
smooth (surface)	**жылма**	dʒılma
soft (~ toys)	**жумшак**	dʒumʃak
solid (~ wall)	**бекем**	bekem
sour (flavor, taste)	**кычкыл**	kıtʃkıl
spacious (house, etc.)	**кең**	keŋ
special (adj)	**атайын**	atajın
straight (line, road)	**түз**	tyz
strong (person)	**күчтүү**	kytʃtyy
stupid (foolish)	**акылсыз**	akılsız
superb, perfect (adj)	**сонун**	sonun
sweet (sugary)	**таттуу**	tattuu
tan (adj)	**күнгө күйгөн**	kyngø kyjgøn
tasty (delicious)	**даамдуу**	daamduu
unclear (adj)	**ачык эмес**	atʃık emes

28. Verbs. Part 1

to accuse (vt)	**айыптоо**	ajıptoo
to agree (say yes)	**макул болуу**	makul boluu

to announce (vt)	кулактандыруу	kulaktandıruu
to answer (vi, vt)	жооп берүү	dʒoop beryy
to apologize (vi)	кечирим суроо	ketʃirim suroo

to arrive (vi)	келүү	kelyy
to ask (~ oneself)	суроо	suroo
to be absent	келбей калуу	kelbej kaluu
to be afraid	жазкануу	dʒazkanuu
to be born	төрөлүү	tørølyy

to be in a hurry	шашуу	ʃaʃuu
to beat (to hit)	уруу	uruu
to begin (vt)	баштоо	baʃtoo
to believe (in God)	ишенүү	iʃenyy
to belong to ...	таандык болуу	taandık boluu
to break (split into pieces)	сындыруу	sındıruu

to build (vt)	куруу	kuruu
to buy (purchase)	сатып алуу	satıp aluu
can (v aux)	жасай алуу	dʒasaj aluu
can (v aux)	жасай алуу	dʒasaj aluu
to cancel (call off)	жокко чыгаруу	dʒokko tʃigaruu

to catch (vt)	кармоо	karmoo
to change (vt)	өзгөртүү	øzgørtyy
to check (to examine)	текшерүү	tekʃeryy
to choose (select)	тандоо	tandoo
to clean up (tidy)	жыйнаштыруу	dʒıjnaʃtıruu

to close (vt)	жабуу	dʒabuu
to compare (vt)	салыштыруу	salıʃtıruu
to complain (vi, vt)	арыздануу	arızdanuu
to confirm (vt)	ырастоо	ırastoo
to congratulate (vt)	куттуктоо	kuttuktoo

to cook (dinner)	тамак бышыруу	tamak bıʃıruu
to copy (vt)	көчүрүү	køtʃyryy
to cost (vt)	туруу	turuu
to count (add up)	саноо	sanoo
to count on ...	... ишенүү	... iʃenyy

to create (vt)	жаратуу	dʒaratuu
to cry (weep)	ыйлоо	ıjloo
to dance (vi, vt)	бийлөө	bijløø
to deceive (vi, vt)	алдоо	aldoo
to decide (~ to do sth)	чечүү	tʃetʃyy

to delete (vt)	жок кылуу	dʒok kıluu
to demand (request firmly)	талап кылуу	talap kıluu
to deny (vt)	тануу, төгүндөө	tanuu, tøgyndøø
to depend on ...	... көзүн кароо	... køzyn karoo
to despise (vt)	киши катарына албоо	kiʃi katarına alboo

to die (vi)	өлүү	ølyy
to dig (vt)	казуу	kazuu
to disappear (vi)	жоголуп кетүү	dʒogolup ketyy
to discuss (vt)	талкуулоо	talkuuloo
to disturb (vt)	тынчын алуу	tıntʃın aluu

29. Verbs. Part 2

to dive (vi)	сүңгүү	syŋgyy
to divorce (vi)	ажырашуу	adʒıraʃuu
to do (vt)	кылуу	kıluu
to doubt (have doubts)	күмөн саноо	kymøn sanoo
to drink (vi, vt)	ичүү	itʃyy

to drop (let fall)	түшүрүп алуу	tyʃyryp aluu
to dry (clothes, hair)	кургатуу	kurgatuu
to eat (vi, vt)	тамактануу	tamaktanuu
to end (~ a relationship)	токтотуу	toktotuu
to excuse (forgive)	кечирүү	ketʃiryy

to exist (vi)	чыгуу	tʃıguu
to expect (foresee)	күтүү	kytyy
to explain (vt)	түшүндүрүү	tyʃyndyryy
to fall (vi)	жыгылуу	dʒıgıluu
to fight (street fight, etc.)	мушташуу	muʃtaʃuu
to find (vt)	таап алуу	taap aluu

to finish (vt)	бүтүрүү	bytyryy
to fly (vi)	учуу	utʃuu
to forbid (vt)	тыюу салуу	tıjɥu saluu
to forget (vi, vt)	унутуу	unutuu
to forgive (vt)	кечирүү	ketʃiryy

to get tired	чарчоо	tʃartʃoo
to give (vt)	берүү	beryy
to go (on foot)	жөө басуу	dʒøø basuu
to hate (vt)	жек көрүү	dʒek køryy

to have (vt)	бар болуу	bar boluu
to have breakfast	эртең менен тамактануу	erteŋ menen tamaktanuu
to have dinner	кечки тамакты ичүү	ketʃki tamaktı itʃyy
to have lunch	түштөнүү	tyʃtønyy

to hear (vt)	угуу	uguu
to help (vt)	жардам берүү	dʒardam beryy
to hide (vt)	жашыруу	dʒaʃıruu
to hope (vi, vt)	үмүттөнүү	ymyttønyy
to hunt (vi, vt)	аңчылык кылуу	aŋtʃılık kıluu
to hurry (vi)	шашуу	ʃaʃuu

to insist (vi, vt)	көшөрүү	køʃøryy
to insult (vt)	кемсинтүү	kemsintyy
to invite (vt)	чакыруу	tʃakıruu
to joke (vi)	тамашалоо	tamaʃaloo
to keep (vt)	сактоо	saktoo

to kill (vt)	өлтүрүү	øltyryy
to know (sb)	таануу	taanuu
to know (sth)	билүү	bilyy
to like (I like …)	жактыруу	dʒaktıruu
to look at …	… кароо	… karoo

to lose (umbrella, etc.)	жоготуу	dʒogotuu
to love (sb)	сүйүү	syjyy
to make a mistake	ката кетирүү	kata ketiryy
to meet (vi, vt)	жолугушуу	dʒoluguʃuu
to miss (school, etc.)	калтыруу	kaltıruu

30. Verbs. Part 3

to obey (vi, vt)	баш ийүү	baʃ ijyy
to open (vt)	ачуу	atʃuu
to participate (vi)	катышуу	katıʃuu
to pay (vi, vt)	төлөө	tøløø
to permit (vt)	уруксат берүү	uruksat beryy

to play (children)	ойноо	ojnoo
to pray (vi, vt)	дуба кылуу	duba kıluu
to promise (vt)	убада берүү	ubada beryy
to propose (vt)	сунуштоо	sunuʃtoo
to prove (vt)	далилдөө	dalildøø
to read (vi, vt)	окуу	okuu

to receive (vt)	алуу	aluu
to rent (sth from sb)	батирге алуу	batirge aluu
to repeat (say again)	кайталоо	kajtaloo
to reserve, to book	камдык буйрутмалоо	kamdık bujrutmaloo
to run (vi)	чуркоо	tʃurkoo

to save (rescue)	куткаруу	kutkaruu
to say (~ thank you)	айтуу	ajtuu
to see (vt)	көрүү	køryy
to sell (vt)	сатуу	satuu
to send (vt)	жөнөтүү	dʒønøtyy
to shoot (vi)	атуу	atuu

to shout (vi)	кыйкыруу	kıjkıruu
to show (vt)	көрсөтүү	kørsøtyy
to sign (document)	кол коюу	kol kojuu
to sing (vi)	сайроо	sajroo

to sit down (vi)	отуруу	oturuu
to smile (vi)	жылмаюу	ʤılmaʤʉu
to speak (vi, vt)	сүйлөө	syjløø
to steal (money, etc.)	уурдоо	uurdoo
to stop (please ~ calling me)	токтотуу	toktotuu
to study (vt)	окуу	okuu
to swim (vi)	сүзүү	syzyy
to take (vt)	алуу	aluu
to talk to ...	... менен сүйлөшүү	... menen syjløʃyy
to tell (story, joke)	айтып берүү	ajtıp beryy
to thank (vt)	ыраазычылык билдирүү	ıraazıtʃılık bildiryy
to think (vi, vt)	ойлоо	ojloo
to translate (vt)	которуу	kotoruu
to trust (vt)	ишенүү	iʃenyy
to try (attempt)	аракет кылуу	araket kıluu
to turn (e.g., ~ left)	бурулуу	buruluu
to turn off	өчүрүү	øtʃyryy
to turn on	күйгүзүү	kyjgyzyy
to understand (vt)	түшүнүү	tyʃynyy
to wait (vt)	күтүү	kytyy
to want (wish, desire)	каалоо	kaaloo
to work (vi)	иштөө	iʃtøø
to write (vt)	жазуу	ʤazuu